The Hebrew Folktale in Premodern Morality Literature

Raphael Patai Series in Jewish Folklore and Anthropology

A complete listing of the books in this series can
be found online at wsupress.wayne.edu.

The Hebrew Folktale in Premodern Morality Literature

VERED TOHAR

Wayne State University Press
Detroit

ISBN 9780814350829 (paperback)
ISBN 9780814347041 (hardcover)
ISBN 9780814347058 (e-book)

Library of Congress Control Number: 2023931099

On cover: The Worms Machzor, Virtzburg 1272, vol. 1, page 2a. Ms. Heb 4° 781/1. Courtesy of the National Library of Israel collection. "Ktiv" Project, the National Library of Israel. Cover design by Mindy Basinger Hill.

Published with support from the fund for the Raphael Patai Series in Jewish Folklore and Anthropology.

All image scans were done with permission from the Rare Book Collection at Bar-Ilan University.

Wayne State University Press rests on Waawiyaataanong, also referred to as Detroit, the ancestral and contemporary homeland of the Three Fires Confederacy. These sovereign lands were granted by the Ojibwe, Odawa, Potawatomi, and Wyandot Nations, in 1807, through the Treaty of Detroit. Wayne State University Press affirms Indigenous sovereignty and honors all tribes with a connection to Detroit. With our Native neighbors, the press works to advance educational equity and promote a better future for the earth and all people.

Wayne State University Press
Leonard N. Simons Building
4809 Woodward Avenue
Detroit, Michigan 48201-1309

Visit us online at wsupress.wayne.edu.

Contents

Acknowledgments vii

Introduction ix

1. Texts, Authors, and Agendas 1

2. The *Musar* Tragedy Tale 15

3. The *Musar* Comedy Tale 37

4. *Musar* Social Exempla 63

5. The Allegorical *Musar* Tale 79

Conclusions and Final Remarks 93

Appendix 1: *Musar* Compilations Cited 101

Appendix 2: Additional *Musar* Tales 107

Notes 115

Bibliography 133

Index of Authors, Themes, Literary Figures, and Terms 145

Index of Biblical and Rabbinic References 151

Index of *Musar* Texts and Primary Sources 153

Index of Tale Types and Motifs 155

Acknowledgments

First and foremost, I would like to thank my teacher, past supervisor, friend, and colleague Rella Kushelevsky, for her professional and emotional support throughout the entire research process. She taught me to follow my beliefs and intuitions, and to look for the unseen, so I might find my own, original research paths.

I would also like to thank Dan Ben-Amos for bolstering my confidence and serving as a supportive sounding-board as I prepared and discovered the thesis of this book. I offer grateful thanks to my teachers, friends, and colleagues: Eli Yassif, Zeev Gries, Noga Rubin, Moshe S. Shoshan, Itamar Drori, Tovi Bibring, Revital Refael-Vivante, Tamar Wolf-Monzon, Dafna Nissim, Claudia Rosenzweig, Marcell Poorthuis, Ilana Rosen, Sara Offenberg, Roni Miron, Peter Lenard, and Chanita Goodblatt.

I am grateful to the Yitzhak Akavayahu Memorial Foundation at Bar-Ilan University for their kind support, which enabled me to publish my research.

Also, I would like to thank Evelyn Grossberg for her editorial support with the first draft of the book, and I am grateful to Ethelea Katzenell for her insightful editing, impeccable English, and bibliographic skills.

I would even like to thank the anonymous readers of the first drafts of the book; their remarks were precious and, certainly, honed and improved my thesis.

The professional staff of Wayne State University Press deserves my thanks for their patience and fine treatment of my texts. I thank Sandra Korn, the acquisition editor, for her kind attitude and professional supervision of the manuscript, Emily Gauronskas for shepherding it through, and Amy Pattullo for copyediting it.

This book was conceived and begun in a secure, routine world, which suddenly transformed into a world besieged by the COVID-19 pandemic. This fact is almost redundant, but it means everything to me. I hope that looking back some four hundred years or more on the achievements of Jewish culture will put this unstable present into better proportion.

Vered Tohar
Lehavim
December 2022

Introduction

Once, a calf that was brought to be slaughtered ran and hid under the prayer shawl of our holy rabbi, who told it: "Go, because that is what you were made for." And it was declared from Heaven: "Since the rabbi is not merciful, we will torment him." And truly, he began to suffer great torments, until his screams were louder than the ruckus made by his herd of horses. But then, he was healed by mercy. One day his maidservant was sweeping the floor and she swept the bugs, killing them. And our holy rabbi said to the maiden: "Let them be, since it is written: 'And His mercy is upon all His works' [Ps. 145:9]." And it was said from Heaven: "Since he is merciful, he merits mercy." And the rabbi was cured.

The tale, "The Rabbi and the Calf," deals with compassion toward all God's creatures and the connection between animals and humans—two themes as surprisingly relevant today as they were legitimate subject matter back in the thirteenth century. This tale was part of *musar* text (a sermon on Jewish morality) that appeared in various versions in premodern Jewish literature. It is found in the chapter on compassion in *Ma'alot ha-Middot* [The degrees of the virtues],[1] in reference to the Babylonian Talmud, *Baba Meṣiah* 85a, but other versions also exist in other compilations, some with some modern adaptations.[2] The actual reason for its appearance in the essay *Ma'alot ha-Middot* is not clear at first reading. What was the function of this tale in its original, nonfiction context, within a didactic sermon on a Jewish virtue? Why was it repeated in the chapter on compassion in *Ma'alot ha-Middot*? Was its use really essential for the author to make his point?

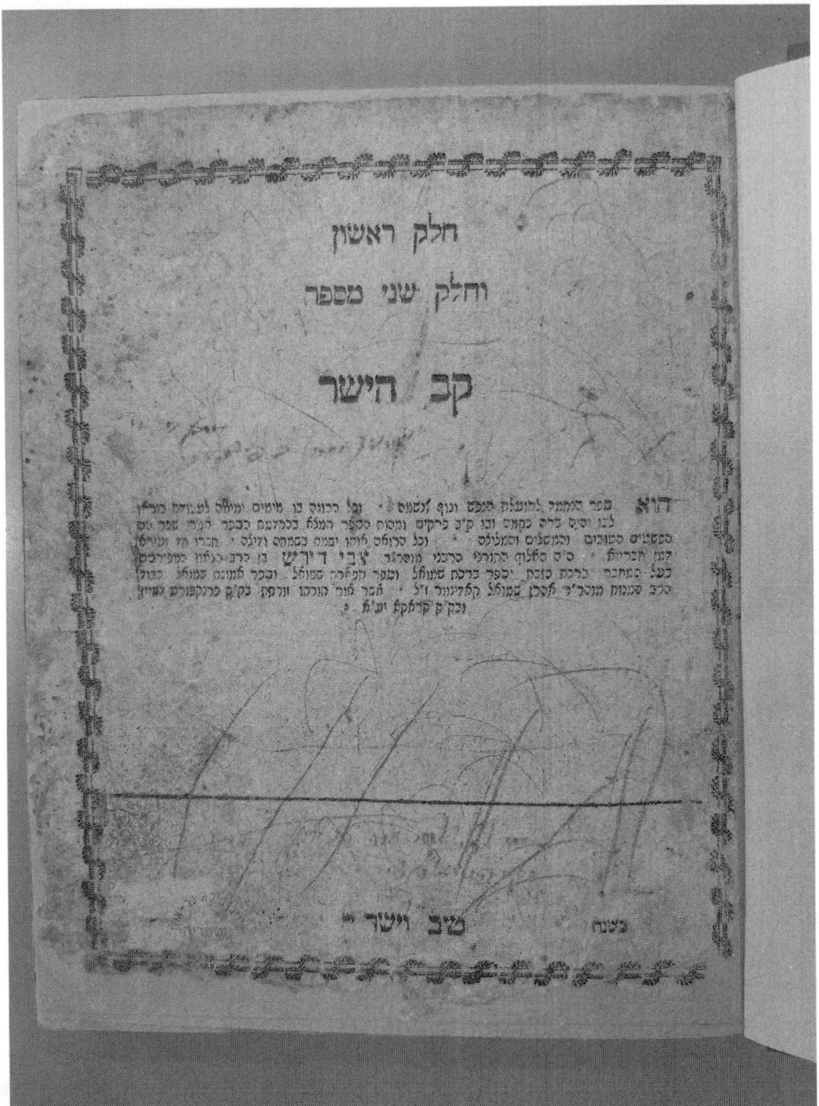

Figure 1. Qav ha-Yashar, Frankfurt 1773, title page. Courtesy of the Rare Book Collection at Bar-Ilan University.

These questions all relate to the subject of the present study, which focuses on the metareading of early modern Jewish *musar* literature written in Hebrew (often with some Aramaic).[3] It examines whether these Jewish folktales were "moralized," so they might fit into the realm of *musar* literature or, perhaps the opposite, that certain moralistic narratives were eventually transformed into folklore.

This pioneer study introduces and analyzes a selection of four hundred published Hebrew folktales found in the corpus of *musar* texts never before intentionally and comprehensively addressed by Jewish literary scholars or folklorists. By means of the analytical reading of these folktales, it is possible to assess their versions and formats, and focus on the renditions that appear in various contexts within the *musar* literature. While this monograph does not contradict the theories presented by prior authors, it suggests the efficacy of rereading these *musar* texts from a different perspective. Thus the discussion considers a triad involving three aspects: the folktale, the ethical *musar* text, and the study of literary genres.

All of the Hebrew folktales discussed here appeared in Jewish *musar* literature printed after the fifteenth century, although some of these tales existed well before the advent of printing. These folktales (as defined below) form the heart and soul of the *musar* literature. Although they are fascinating, they have never been, strangely enough, the subjects of any in-depth studies such as is offered here. The extensive research done toward the publication of this book suggests that, during the period extending from the early sixteenth to the early eighteenth centuries, certain Jewish folktales were combined together and moralized to serve as special didactic, ethical allegories, tools for rabbinic teachings about vices and virtues.[4]

Some of this printed *musar* literature was authored in the medieval era and preserved in handwritten manuscripts until eventually being printed; it was and still remains the spiritual food of many Hebrew readers across the Jewish world.[5] Owing to the printing industry, which Jewish culture embraced from the very beginning of the print era, *musar* books were widely circulated across the globe, east and west, and were easily accessible. Along with other canonic Jewish texts—the Bible, the Mishnah, the

Talmud, and the Mahzor (festival prayer book)—they were soon found on many Jewish bookshelves.[6] Hence, apart from communicating didactic messages, this literature became a conveyer of folkloric traditions and especially avenues for preserving Jewish folktales.[7]

The following pages introduce a selection of folktales taken from the printed *musar* corpus, sorted into four distinct genres, in accordance with their content and literary foci, by means of modern approaches to folktale studies (formalistic, comparative, and semiotic readings). These are accompanied by examples demonstrating their significance in the context of Hebrew *musar* literature.[8] The study aims to turn the attention of folklorists and scholars of Jewish studies to the narrative component of early modern *musar* books. Various genres of Jewish folktales are included in almost every sermon or *musar* text, where they have a very meaningful role. The insertion of such allegorical folktales into the *musar* literature, the reasons for their inclusions, and their impact on the messages of the texts have significance for the study of folklore in general as well as for understanding the nature and function of the *musar* texts.

Creating a new corpus of texts was the first goal of this research, to fill a significant lacuna in regard to Jewish folktales. While Jewish folklore studies have discussed biblical, rabbinic, and even medieval tales, no serious consideration has been given to those folktales embedded in the *musar* literature. This book thus presents novel research on a distinct and previously neglected category of folktales.

To do this it was necessary to distinguish *musar* literature from other types of Jewish writing, and this is done by means of two criteria, the former internal and the latter external: 1) the content of *musar* texts deals primarily with ethical concepts and moral conduct, morality being at the center of the discussion, and 2) the texts under consideration were commonly accepted as belonging to the *musar* category of Jewish literature by their original readers, when first published, and are still considered as such by Jewish scholars today. Using these criteria, numerous *musar* publications were examined to locate embedded folktales.

This new category of folktales opens many possibilities for future study in the fields of Jewish ethics, Jewish philology, Hebrew and Aramaic linguistics, and more. These are beyond the scope of this study, but the first steps are laid in crystalizing the *musar* category.

The folktales are defined and characterized here as a group by their literary themes and genres. This literary analysis stage in the research process provided some crucial observations. It was found that the *musar* folktales may be classified into four distinct genres: tragedy, comedy, social exemplum (parable), and theological allegory. They run the gamut from happy to tragic, reflecting on a full range of human experience: personal relationships with God and relationships between individuals, divine reward and divine punishment, mundane life on Earth and incorporeal afterlife. The embedded *musar* folktales reflect all the human themes found in the literary contexts in which they appear—adventure, family, marriage, parenthood, sovereignty, education, faith, livelihood—not specifically limited to Jewish topics.

Moreover, all of these folktales also fit into one of four complementary, antonymic themes: loyalty and betrayal, love and hate, good and evil, life and death. The authors of these works, as well as their readers, probably were not aware of these genres, nor did they did see the distinction between fictional and nonfictional prose within the same text as being significant in the *musar* context. As Alan Dundes noted, folktales in general provide a more familiar and acceptable format for the readership to receive the authors' ethical message. After all, those premodern authors were intent on presenting guidelines toward an ideal Jewish way of life. Keeping the example systematic would have been a useful strategy.[9]

Another insight was that the folktales that *musar* authors included in their works delineated a balance between unacceptable behavior, transgressions and sins versus normative behavior, good deeds, and observance of the mitzvoth (commandments), by presenting exaggerated situations and unlikely occurrences. These rhetorical and poetic techniques were designed to frighten their readers and to convince them to change their "habitus" (perception and attitudes) and, consequently, their conduct.[10] This, of course, was an outcome of the belief that habitual reading has this kind of transformative potential; as such, these *musar* folktales, exaggerated as they are, with their systematic structures, might have swayed Jewish readers to become better Jews.

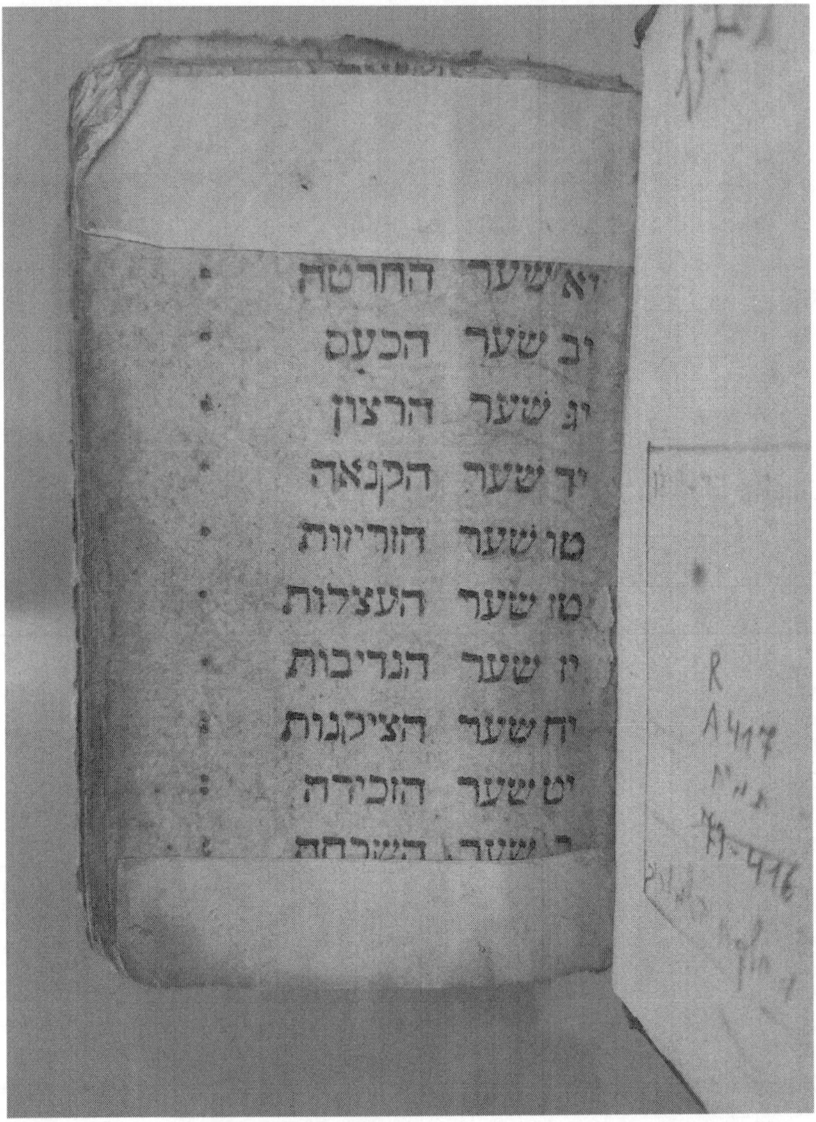

Figure 2. Orḥot Ṣaddiqim, Sulzbach 1688, table of contents. Courtesy of the Rare Book Collection at Bar-Ilan University.

An additional finding culled from this novel corpus is that many of the tales appear repeatedly in a number of the *musar* books, indicating that the authors of the *musar* literature referred to and influenced one another. They lived in what Stanley Fish called "one big virtual community," a virtual readership community, such that their texts commonly referred to prior *musar* works. These *musar* authors were familiar with the corpus of existing *musar* literature and were part of a long literary tradition striving for public consensus. It was not an experimental literary format, nor were they trying to create avant-garde literature; they knew what their readers expected and met those expectations.

Although the genre of *musar* literature flourished and was fostered by a wide consensus, nonetheless it did not interact with other Jewish cultural literature, despite its alleged basis in familiar folktales. In other words, the *musar* literature had an exclusive repertoire of some dozens of folktales, which were frequently used but not usually included in other types of Hebrew story compilations and anthologies. *Musar* texts do not have much in common with belletristic works, meant to be read in leisure time and focused on entertainment and the beauty of the artistic expression. The two are very different literary forms and they do not seem to talk to one another in any significant way.

It was also surprising to find that none of the authors' epilogues to the *musar* works (where they have one) specifically refers to the folktales embedded within them. This seemed inconsistent with their common contention that they were influenced by other *musar* works, by philosophical writings, and by oral learning and knowledge that they had acquired over the years. None of them refers to the embedded tales as being "folktales," nor to the fact that a very significant part of each *musar* text consisted of tens of such tales. It seems that neither the authors nor the readership were aware of such literary terms. Perhaps the *musar* authors inserted the folktales to add appeal to their narratives; but they avoided acknowledging that their didactic works were also entertaining. Clearly, this is a fertile topic for scholars, to investigate how the *musar* texts were really compiled.

Since there are too many *musar* folktales to present to the English reader in this book, a small representative sample was selected to provide a glimpse of the typical genres, themes, motifs, protagonists, conflicts, and resolutions. These tales have been taken out of their original contexts, which may be considered problematic in certain research paradigms, especially when dealing with the subject of morality. The preliminary assumption behind this objection is that this was not done due to the folktales' intrinsic aesthetic value, but rather because they serve as allegories representing broader ideas. Though these folktales cannot be fully understood without their contexts, *musar* authors decided to insert them into new contexts, to bolster the contents of their new messages. On the other hand, taking those tales out of the *musar* context enabled me to emphasize their poetic features.

The selected folktales, as they appear in this work, were all taken from Hebrew *musar* texts and translated into standard modern American English; some explanations were added so that English-speaking readers could better understand them. Every translation is, by its very nature, an interpretation of sorts, a rendering of one culture in terms of another culture, but that is a problem every researcher deals with when publishing a scholarly work in a language other than that of the original text. Since Hebrew was not a living, spoken language in the early modern period, the phrasing of ideas was not entirely free and natural; in fact, premodern Hebrew (and Aramaic) is often quite unintelligible today, even for native Hebrew speakers (somewhat like Shakespearean texts to native English speakers). Under these circumstances, a choice was made to give the English reader the essence of the plot rather than a more exact translation.

The book begins by providing some background on the whole group of source texts we now call *musar* literature. This literary genre, its authors, and its contexts are presented in chapter 1.

Chapter 2 presents a discussion of one *musar* genre, tragedy, in which the tale describes the main character's deteriorating welfare and happiness. This character embodies poor judgment and bad conduct, a deficient habitus, clearly deserving of punishment. The *musar* tragedy's plot ends in disaster from the protagonist's perspective, which is, obviously, consistent with the ethos of Jewish culture and confirms the values espoused in the *musar* text.

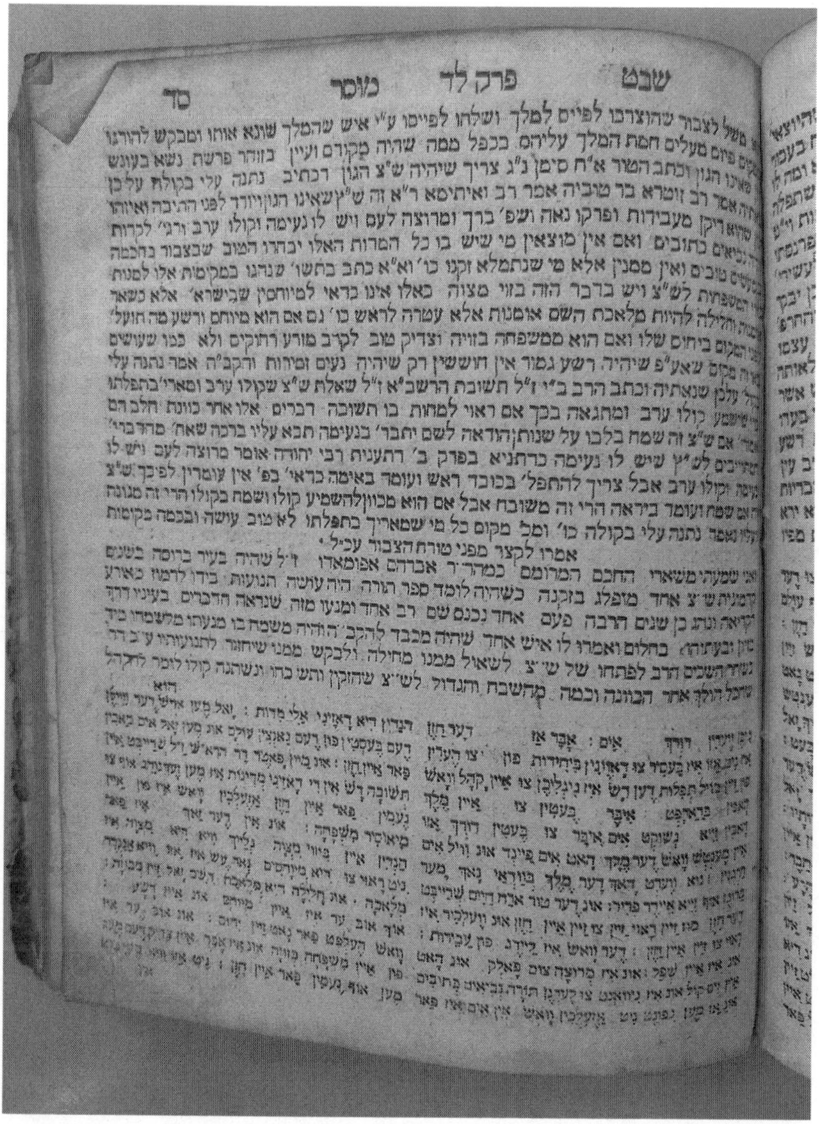

Figure 3. Sheveṭ Musar, Sudylkiv 1821, tale. Courtesy of the Rare Book Collection at Bar-Ilan University.

Chapter 3 presents the *musar* comedy, where the plot describes the progressive personal growth and increasing welfare and happiness of the protagonist. The *musar* comedy has a happy ending, that is, an ending consistent with the ethos of Jewish culture, one that reaffirms the values of Jewish society.

Chapter 4 deals with ethicosocial exempla, which are tales that emphasize a special or very unusual behavior of the main character.[11] The Jewish folktales in this genre relate specifically to anonymous protagonists and present short anecdotes from everyday life, especially about social dilemmas. Allegedly secular, universal, and neutral in regard to theological implications, they relate to social issues without any direct reference to religious matters. Such tales are meant to direct the reader's attention to common, everyday situations having the potential to cause harm or to be beneficial, depending on the actions of the protagonists, thus revealing the Jewish social agenda.

Chapter 5 discusses theological allegories. These tales are rooted in theodicy (the problem of evil in the context of God's omnipotence) and focus on the relationship between God and humans. The legends included here are shaped as allegories, constructed around a fixed group of protagonists, usually a king and his servants, who represent God and his believers. Such legends are meant to fulfill a human fantasy, to provide insight into God's will and divine justice; they purport to provide the readers access to the secrets of the world.

The conclusion presents a panoramic view of the *musar* folktale corpus in light of the printing revolution, its impact on the dissemination of the folktales, and its creation of communities of readers across the Jewish Diaspora.

1

TEXTS, AUTHORS, AND AGENDAS

Musar texts feature a blend of religious ethos, cultural and social conventions, and the individual style of each specific author, and they were clearly designed to meet readers' expectations. The *musar* authors of the texts in this study took on the role of public spokespersons, becoming the voices of their societies, in accordance with a tacit agreement made between the authors, the community leaders, the publishers, and the readership.[1] In fact, the Jewish authors of premodern *musar* texts represented the religious authorities.

These authors knew that their works had the potential to produce a strong impact on the readership. As such, they served as messengers or agents, trying to deliver ethical messages as well as possible in a pleasing literary style; they wanted to capture the hearts of their readers, in a novel yet conventional way. The *musar* text was not an experimental work, nor a place for groundbreaking ideas, but rather an effort to present very familiar, traditional theological materials in the most appealing manner.[2] Thus, the authors of *musar* texts were much like the narrators of the folktales, standing on very familiar ground and dealing with well-known materials. But they were able to get the readers' attention by presenting familiar ideas in the novel way of including folktales in their texts.[3] Take, for example, the tale "The Prisoner," found in a talmudic tractate entitled *Yesh Noḥalin* (There are those who inherit), a tractate that warns against underestimation, although the tale itself might suggest the opposite since it emphasizes the gap between physical conditions of life and a spiritual state of mind.[4]

> **Once there was** a physician who was imprisoned by the king and put in a cell as narrow as a grave. And he was bound up in iron chains around his arms and around his neck, was dressed in very coarse woolen rags, and given only barley bread with a spoon of salt to eat and some water. The king ordered the guards to listen to the words he uttered while in prison, since the physician was very wise. But the prisoner would not talk for many days. The king then let the physician's relatives visit him, thinking that perhaps he would talk to them. When his relatives came to visit, they were astonished by the happiness that was evident on his face, despite his poor conditions. They said to him with great wonder: "How is it that your face is glowing, your flesh is still not gaunt, and your strength has not disappeared? How is it that you are in such good condition after all this time in prison?" And the physician answered them: "Every day, I take a special potion made of seven ingredients and it keeps me alive and well." And the visitors answered: "Please tell us the ingredients, so that when others of us are arrested, we shall know how to protect ourselves." The physician answered: The first ingredient is faith in God, who keeps evil away from me. The second is hope. The third is the understanding that I'm being punished for something wrong I surely did. The fourth is the knowledge that there's nothing I can do about it, so I should just accept my situation. The fifth is knowing that my suffering in this life is penance for the afterlife. The sixth is that I know that things could be worse, and others suffer more than I, so I'm grateful for what I have in prison—clothes and food and a roof over my head. The seventh is that I know that God will save me, relieve my suffering, and will punish my enemies.

This folktale exemplifies confidence in the power and justice of God, the personal strength of the true believer, and the expectation of readers to find an illustrative tale within a *musar* text. Perfect for all these purposes, an embedded *musar* tale both entertains and reaffirms the cultural ethos. Moreover, it includes distant echoes of ancient folktales constructed around the same theme—the optimist who finds the good in any situation.[5] Such a personality is encountered in the Talmud in the figure of R. Naḥum Ish Gamzu, who remained optimistic in the face of all of his many troubles.[6] That a similar theme can be found in a rabbinic source enhances the Jewish reader's sense of identification with the protagonist; repeated motifs give the impression that this is the fate of the Jewish people throughout the generations (although this specific tale is somewhat optimistic). There is a lot of suffering and horror throughout this simple plot, more than the author was willing to make explicit. A single tale never stands alone but is a unique expression in a chain of similar messages.[7] Thus the folktales one finds in *musar* texts are surprisingly much bolder and more daring than one would expect to find in *musar* narratives, which accounts for their powerful impact and distinctive appeal.[8]

Yet the voices aired beyond the folktales in the corpus are neither uniform nor necessarily harmonious. However, that is the very quality that enables the folktales to find a place in different literary and cultural contexts. Indeed, that is why it is worthwhile to look back and to examine the various literary and ideological sources of these folktales in a few of the main collections in the Christian medieval world, as well as to examine the contexts in which they are embedded.

Two Latin folktale anthologies not only became bestsellers in their day, but also continued to influence European literature for hundreds of years following their initial publication dates, essentially creating a very important reservoir of literary themes that later amassed many versions in all the contemporary vernaculars. The impact of these collected tales was significant, touching the medieval Hebrew tales and even Western literary tradition.

The first of these is *Disciplina Clericalis* (Teaching the clerics), a Latin twelfth-century compilation of thirty-three tales composed by Petrus Alphonsi. The author was a Spanish Jewish physician and writer formerly named Moses Sephardi, who had converted to Christianity. He was born in Islamic Spain, and after his conversion he spent most of his life in England and France. The *Disciplina Clericalis* is inspired and influenced by Arab morality and literary tradition, such as *The Arabian Nights*, and was adapted to suit Christian readers, but it also influenced Jewish narrative tradition. Tales like "The Half Friend" and "The Two Clerics Who Entered a Tavern" are well known in medieval Hebrew narrative tradition, with slight variations. This book was translated into all the contemporary vernacular languages and was printed in many editions. Actually, it was one of the greatest bestsellers in medieval Europe. The first scholarly edition of this work was produced by Friedrich Wilhelm Schmidt in 1827.[9]

Although the original thirty-three tales in the *Disciplina Clericalis* do not explicitly appear in my collection of *musar* tales, nonetheless the worldview they express and confirm regarding the cosmic order—that evil doers are punished, that the good are rewarded, and other popular wisdom—also seeped into the tales embedded in the Jewish *musar* literature.[10]

Around the end of the thirteenth century or the start of the fourteenth, the anonymous *Gesta Romanorum* (Deeds of the Romans) was published in Europe, which was also an anthology of ethical fables in Latin. It had a variety of sources, both Asian and European. Each tale opened with the mention of the name of a Roman Caesar, frequently fictitious, but perhaps this inspired the choice of the collection's title. This book eventually became one of the sources of inspiration for Chaucer, Boccaccio, and other authors of folktale collections in Italian, French, and English. Even William Shakespeare and the Romantic poets, such as Friedrich Schiller, are thought to have been inspired by its tales. Manuscripts of the *Gesta Romanorum* and various other copies are not entirely identical, since the structure of this folktale compilation allowed the copyists to omit or add tales relatively freely.

At the start of the printing age, the *Gesta Romanorum* was first printed both in Utrecht and in Cologne, although both the publication dates and the publisher's names remain uncertain. Later on, this work was published in many editions and was translated into the various vernaculars.[11] Eli Yassif mentions this work as being part of the heritage of the exemplum genre that had a large influence on the Hebrew folktale.[12] Research studies are still being written about it, proving the broad scope of its impact on European literature both in the Middle Ages and at the outset of the modern age.[13]

In addition to these external sources, worthy of mention are also two key Jewish cultural works that have also laid foundations for the Jewish *musar* literature. The first one is a manuscript entitled *Midrash 'Aseret ha-Dibrot'*, which is one of the most important and thoroughly researched Hebrew folktale collections in Hebrew culture. It was apparently created in the region of Babylonia during the age of the *Ge'onim* (scholars who served as the presidents of the Babylonian Talmud academies), from where it was disseminated, by means of copies, westward to Ashkenaz (Germany and northern France), and all of Europe. In the nineteenth century, it was also found in Yemenite script and in North Africa. Notable about this manuscript is that it may be the first example of a collection of Hebrew tales gathered for the purpose of recreational reading, despite the fact that it contains *musar* tales, the goal of which was to encourage its readers to observe the Ten Commandments of Judaism and to beware of breaking them.

We have no signed, original copy, merely those copied manuscripts that survived from thirteenth-century Ashkenaz. Actually, this work contains an indeterminate number of tales clustered together under ten chapter headings, in accordance with the Ten Commandments. For each commandment, at some level or another, suitable tales were selected that would strengthen or confirm its significance. Between the various handwritten copies, there is a large degree of difference regarding the number of tales in the anthology, their order in the text, and even in the rendition of the tale.[14]

The second anthology, *Ḥibbur Yafeh meha-Yeshu'ah* (An elegant composition concerning relief after adversity)[15] is an eleventh-century collection of tales compiled by R. Nissim b. Jacob Ga'on from Kairouan (in today's Tunisia). It is likely that this collection was originally written in Judeo-Arabic script, but later on, when it was disseminated in Europe, it was translated into Hebrew. The original Judeo-Arabic manuscript was lost, and what remains in the hands of researchers is a much later Judeo-Arabic manuscript[16] and various Hebrew translations.[17] This work stands out in comparison to the other medieval folktale collections, since, unlike the others, this author's name is known.[18] The purpose of these *musar* tales was to teach Jewish ethics in the style of the Arabic *ādāb* (belles lettres) from the eighth and ninth centuries, so R. Nissim Ga'on used these tales, embedding them into his text, under the influence of his Muslim surroundings. The work was modeled after the exemplar of the Arab literary genre, entitled *Al-faraj ba'd al-shiddah* (The salvation after the hardship), that had been popular from the beginning of the eighth century. The author identified with this work is Abu 'Ali al-Muḥassin al-Tanūkhī; it is only in manuscript form and no other copy is available.[19] According to Yassif, the uniqueness of this anthology is that all the tales in it stand alone as distinct, separate units, and the collection has no unifying or connecting textual framework.[20] According to Kushelevsky, all these folktales originated in Ashkenazic regions. Most of these parables provide a theological or social moral lesson and stress the values of retribution (*lex talionis*): reward and punishment, in this life or the afterlife.[21]

In this study, the texts under discussion are classified into six main categories, as follows:[22]

The *historical period* in which the text was originally composed: medieval literature (e.g., *Tiqun Middot ha-Nefesh* [Rectifying the moral qualities of the soul] by Ibn Gabirol); and premodern literature (e.g., *Qav ha-yashar* by Kaidanover). Modern literature (e.g., *Ma'amarei ha-Re'iyah* [The Writings of Avraham Yitzchak Hakohen Kook]) is outside the scope of this work.

The *language of the original text*: Hebrew (e.g., *Ṣava'at ha-Ramban* [The Ramban's will] by R. Moses b. Naḥman, a.k.a. Naḥmanides); Yiddish (e.g., *Brandshpiegel* [Burning mirror] by R. Moshe b. Ḥanokh Altshuler); Ladino (e.g., *Yalquṭ me'Am Lo'ez* [Anthology from a foreign people] by R. Ya'akov Culi); and Judeo-Arabic (e.g., *Ḥibbur Yafeh meha-Yeshu'ah* [An elegant compilation concerning relief after adversity] by R. Nissim b. Jacob Ga'on).[23]

The *author's geographical origin*: Ashkenaz (e.g., *Sefer Ḥasidim* [The book of the pious] compiled by R. Judah b. Samuel of Regensburg, a.k.a. Yehudah he-Ḥasid, or Judah the Pious); the Balkans (e.g., *Pele yo'eṣ* [Wonderful advisor] by R. Eliezer Papo); before the 1492 expulsion of the Jews from Spain and Portugal (e.g., *Ḥovot ha-Levavot* [The duties of the hearts] by Ibn Paquda); Italy (e.g., *Nofet ṣufim* [Sweet honey] by R. Judah Messer Leon); the Land of Israel (e.g., *Sefer Ḥasidim* [The book of the pious, or those who have fear] by R. El'azar b. Moshe Azikri); North Africa (e.g., *Eṣ haim* [Tree of life] by Jacob Israel Ḥagiz); Yemen (e.g., the anonymous *Sefer ha-ma'alot* [The book of steps]); Iraq (e.g., *Ma'aseh Nissim* [A miraculous tale] by R. Shelomoh Bekhor Ḥuṣin) among others.

The *mode of distribution*: printed (e.g., *Menorat ha-Ma'or* [Shining candelabra] by Isaac Aboab); never published in print (e.g., most of the chapters of *Menorat ha-Ma'or* by Israel b. Joseph Alnaqua); often copied before and after it was printed (e.g., the anonymous *Orḥot Ṣaddiqim* [The ways of the righteous]); a work that received secondary citations (e.g., the anonymous *Midrash 'Aseret ha-Dibrot'* [Commentary of the ten statements]).

The existence of *contemporary academic recognition*, manifested by the source's publication in a scientific edition or its inclusion in electronic databases or some other form of information retrieval and storage (e.g., *Sefer Lev Ṭov* [Book of the good heart] by Isaac b. Eliakim of Posen); or as part of an accredited university syllabus (e.g., the popular Yiddish *Ṣe'enah u-re'enah*, titled in full *Hamishah humshe Torah 'im kol ha-haftarot bi leshon Ashkenaz: Se'enah u-re'enah* [Five books of the Torah in the language of Ashkenaz: Go out and see] by Jacob b. Isaac Ashkenazi of Janów Lubelski).[24]

The *subject of the text*: animal stories (e.g., *Mashal ha-Qadmoni* [The parable of the ancient one] by Isaac b. Solomon Ibn Sahula); ethical wills and last wills and testaments (e.g., *Ṣava'at R. Yehudah ha-Nasi* [The will of R. Judah ha-Nasi]); commentaries on the Pentateuch and Jewish scrolls (e.g., *Or ha-ḥayyim* [The light of life] by Ḥayyim b. Mosheh ibn 'Aṭṭar);[25] didactic legends (e.g., the anonymous *Ḥibbur ha-ma'asiyot* [Collection of tales]); moral instruction regarding human nature (e.g., *Ṣemaḥ ṣaddiq* [Righteous growth] by R. Leon of Modena); hagiographic literature (e.g., as found in *Sefer Ḥasidim*); travelogues (e.g., *Ma'agal ṭov* [A good round-trip] by R. Ḥayyim Yosef David Azulai), and so on.

The contents of these six basic categories, relying as they do on descriptive classifications, suggest the great internal diversity of the texts, while the large numbers of publications within each category supports their extensive external impact. Furthermore, the popular nature of such *musar* books was assured, as Ze'ev Gries points out, by their simplicity of expression, the motivation of the *musar* authors to reach as large a readership as possible, as well as the catalytic effect produced by the advent of printing on book circulation. From his perspective, the main research challenge is the "colorfulness" of this wide range of texts and their manifold manifestations. Taking account of the particularities of individual texts, Gries focuses on the demands of those texts and addresses the methodological difficulties imposed by the broad delineation of *musar* literature.[26]

Ethical literature, which is an ancient group of texts, is a universal cultural product. Every literate culture, every literate religion, developed and continues to develop a collection of such texts.[27] Due to the close connection between morality and didacticism, almost every classical or medieval work was designed to teach the reader a lesson.[28] But particular to this study is its focus on a corpus of *musar* folktales; thus in many ways it continues and completes earlier studies by Eli Yassif, Dan Ben-Amos, and Rella Kushlevsky, each of whom has offered a different perspective on certain Hebrew folktale anthologies consisting of various texts from specific periods of time. Among his other works, Yassif published academic editions of *Sefer ha-zikhronot: Hu divrē ha-yamim li-yeraḥmi'el* (MS Jerusalem 8°3182), and the article *Meshalim shel Shlomoh ha-Melekh [Fables of King Solomon].*[29] Dan Ben-Amos annotated academic editions in English of *Mimekor Yisrael*[30] and translated stories that are part of the Haifa Collection of Israeli Folktales. Rella Kushelevsky authored an academic and annotated edition of *Sefer ha-ma'asim* [The book of deeds].[31]

Figure 4. Sha'arē Teshuvah, Lemberg 1847, title page. Courtesy of the Rare Book Collection at Bar-Ilan University.

But in spite of all those important works, the connection between Jewish *musar* literature and Jewish folktales has not yet received the academic attention it deserves.[32] For many reasons, scholars of Jewish folklore have paid scant attention to the corpus of *musar* prose, although it holds a significant place in both medieval and premodern Jewish culture.[33] *Musar* authors generally used folktales to emphasize and illustrate abstract concepts.[34] It is hard to find a Jewish *musar* book that does not season the ethical text with folktales. But the interpretations of those folktales usually accommodate the focal ideas being promoted in each specific context. This cultural phenomenon occurs due to the nature of folktales since they are flexible enough to enable multiple manifestations and interpretations.[35]

The widespread cultural phenomenon of the circulation and acceptance of some Jewish medieval and premodern *musar* works suggests that, like other folk materials, they are adaptable and, as such, have many kindred versions. In addition, the contents and textual features of these texts—having a plain style and contents, meant to be clear and memorable—are similar to those found in international folk literature. In fact, Dan, Yassif, and Gries approach *musar* books as folk literature, even though they are prepared texts and often have a known author. Viewing a *musar* book as a complex of arenas, that is, as a heterogenic space, is crucial to the full understanding of the Jewish approach to a work that conveys cultural values along with poetic additions.[36] This scholarly trend to read *musar* as folklore originated in the early work of Shmuel Werses, in particular his pioneering doctoral dissertation, in which he defined Sephardic *musar* literature as a literary genre with folkloric elements designed to provide practical instructions for the life of the individual and society.[37]

These folktales seem to create a balance with the nonfictional, idealistic texts, by simulating the true essence of life, illustrating the purportedly "realistic" conduct of "real" people with "real" human weaknesses. Each tale was designed to counter the unambiguousness of the ethical text, serving as the place for the questionable, and exposing the unexpected, nonconformist, and even perverse. Furthermore, these folktales were included to capture the readers' attention by being surprising or evoking excitement or astonishment. They were crafted to arouse emotional responses, to ensure that the nonfictional prose would be remembered.

Reading an ethical text rife with folktales is like trying to cross a river with protruding rocks. The stream of fast-flowing water represents the ethics, phrased as nonnarrative prose. One must be quite skilled to successfully cross to the other side quickly, with dexterity. If the current is too strong, it cannot be crossed it at all. Someone unskilled or slow and cautious might jump from one stable rock to another, to feel the confidence instilled by the sensation of standing on solid ground. The embedded folktales serve as the rocks in the ethical stream.

The didactic frame and telos of these texts sometimes even justified the inclusion of certain very outrageous folktales. While the general framing of the *musar* works was conservative, the contents of the embedded tales might be revolutionary or provocative; such tales are highlighted below. Ethical texts provided fertile soil for some bold and venturesome folktales, while the entire conservative structure of the work acts as a sort of safety valve for the readers; both the wildness of the tale and the reader's anxiety are constrained by its didactic frame. In effect, *musar* texts serve as gatekeepers, accommodating the presence of riotous plots. The embedded folktales are metaphorical road maps to help the readers find their way home—to the place where a good Jew belongs.

"The Lentils and the Pumpkins," which we find in chapter 22 on modesty in Luzzatto's *Mesillat Yesharim*, can serve as an example of a dialogue between the conservative and the provocative.

Once, there was a man who came to the Land of Israel from Babylon and married an Israelite woman. One time, he asked her to cook him two lentils, meaning that she cooks a small quantity of lentils. But she literally cooked only two lentils and he was furious. After this, he asked her to cook a lot of lentils and she made an enormous pot of lentils, more than one could eat. Then, he told her to go to the market and bring back two pumpkins—but he used the Babylonian name for pumpkins, which was *bozina*; but in the Land of Israel, *bozina* is a candle. So, she brought him two candles instead of two pumpkins.

This folktale was taken from the Babylonian Talmud, *Nedarim* 66b, where it is found in the midst of a discussion about bad wives and the question of coping with a bad marriage. But in *Mesillat Yesharim*, the tale is told to demonstrate the husband's humility is a virtue, for he is bearing with his wife's stupidity. If we ignore the context, this is actually a tale about a misunderstanding between alien cultures, a joke, an anecdote on the difference between the literal meaning of speech and about not understanding subtexts.[38] All along, the reader is not sure whether the wife really does not understand the instructions or is doing these foolish things on purpose, acting like a fool, and the tale has the inner structure of a fool's tale.[39] But when we assess the tale in the didactic context of *Mesillat Yesharim*, it has a very different meaning, becoming a story about a bold woman who is not afraid to humiliate her husband. It is also a story about the difficulty of a man and a woman from different cultures having a peaceful marriage. It cautions men about foreign women and teaches women how to oppose their husbands. This provocative tone is an outcome of a deconstructive reading, delicately implied in the text. Whether the readers notice those radical nuances or not, the potential for this kind of interpretation is, nonetheless, present.

The tension created in this case is not the outcome of taking the folktale out of its original context, which was common practice in medieval folktale anthologies. It arises instead from the author's felt need to insert a folktale into the middle of his ethical text in the first place. Thus the question, whether the tale is crucial or marginal to the texture of the work as a whole, is a major consideration. Indeed, what can the reader learn from it?

The inclusion of folktales in Jewish ethical literature is clearly not an exclusively Jewish phenomenon, since such tales are also found in Arabic, Latin, French, and other ethical literatures. Folktales and moral contents appeared together everywhere; nevertheless, the *musar* literature has a special repertoire, which is often repeated within the *musar* corpus. Certain folkloric plots circulated around the *musar* works, which is not surprising in light of the fact that there was a commonality of topics. A folktale embedded in a *musar* text was widely disseminated and very visible. Popular Jewish texts, especially those that survived the medieval era

Figure 5. Hovot ha-Levavot, Constantinople 1550, title page. Courtesy of the Rare Book Collection at Bar-Ilan University.

and, subsequently, appeared in print, became an inherent part of Jewish culture, and their embedded folktales have been preserved in the collective Jewish cultural memory.

This is not to say that one does not find folktales in other important texts: literary anthologies, autobiographies, homilies, commentaries, and so on. However, the present folklore research is historically limited to the folktales found in printed *musar* literature from 1480 to 1800, the period in which the print industry changed the face of Jewish culture. The discussion here ends at the beginning of the nineteenth century, just before works from *Ḥasidism* (pietistic, mystic Judaism) and the *Haskalah* (the Jewish Enlightenment movement) found their way into the literary field and changed it, yet again.

The following chapters present the four genres of *musar* folktales found in premodern Hebrew *musar* texts. Chapter 2 focuses on *musar* tragedy.

2

THE *MUSAR* TRAGEDY TALE

It seems that *musar* and tragedy go well together, because both approach life in a severe manner, dealing with the nature of sin and punishment, evil and condemnation. This study considers the *musar* tragedy as a way of telling a story that has the worst possible ending for the main protagonist—although, from the reader's point of view, the ending is definitely a good one. In other words, a tale that concludes with an evil protagonist being severely punished, as justice dictates, is an outcome that readers accept as a good resolution, despite the negative impact on the literary figure, whose fate is bad. The disparity between the position of the main character in a *musar* tragedy and the attitude of the readership is what makes it so appealing and effective.[1]

The formula of the *musar* tragedy, as may be seen throughout this corpus, is as follows. In terms of the literary structure, the plot moves from a high point to a low point in regard to the situation of the protagonist; that is, the story describes a decline with respect to the protagonist's welfare and happiness. As to the social context, the plot ends with a disaster from the perspective of the main character; however, it is consistent with the ethos of Jewish culture, which is confirmed by the values espoused in the *musar* text. That is, whenever a protagonist displays poor conduct or character, he or she meets the deserved punishment.

Table 1. The Structure of the *Musar* Tragedy

	Beginning	Middle	End	Outcome
Main character in action	Coping with temptation or a bad trait	Committing a sin or behaving badly	Undergoing divine or community punishment	Adhering to the format of the tragedy genre
The reader	Awareness of the problematic situation	Understanding that the main character must be punished	Accepting the punishment	Reaffirming Jewish cultural values

The scheme shown in table 1 describes the flow of the *musar* tragedy, marking the plot and the reactions of the readers, who go through a didactic process as they follow the experiences of the main character.

The Virgin Who Gouged Out Her Eyes

The tale of "The Virgin Who Gouged Out Her Eyes," in which the female protagonist is compelled to commit self-mutilation, is found in *Ṣemaḥ ṣaddiq*, in the chapter on modesty.

> Once, in a certain city, there lived a chaste and pious maiden, who did not wish to engage in the vanities of worldly pleasures. The ruler of the city saw her and desired her, so he sent secret emissaries to talk to her, but when he was unable to persuade her to come to him, he decided to take her by force. He went to her house accompanied by a large contingent and took her to his home. When she saw that her screams and cries went unheeded, she asked him what it was about her that caused him to desire her more than all the other maidens. He answered: "Your lovely eyes hold me spellbound." She then said to him: "Now that I've seen that you love my eyes so fiercely, I'll comply with your wishes. Just let me prepare myself for a while in a private room, and afterwards, I'll do as you wish." The ruler then ordered that she be brought to a room. She closed the

door, took a knife and gouged out both her eyes—and then opened the door and said to him: "Since you love my eyes so much, here they are in your hands. You may do with them as you wish." Shocked and surprised, the ruler sent her away. She went home and lived out her days chaste and modest.

In this gory *musar* tale, we see that the maiden, when faced with having to choose between being raped by a repugnant suitor and mutilating herself, prefers to disfigure herself and live out her life in isolation. Only by destroying that which attracted this tenacious suitor to her would he reject her as she had rejected him. The connection between gouging out one's eyes and forbidden sexual desire is an ancient one in Western culture; as Freud noted, gouging out one's eyes symbolizes self-castration, from which it follows that looking at an object of sexual desire embodies the idea of engaging in the sexual act.[2]

In the tradition of the Greek tragedy, we have the story of Oedipus, who gouges out his own eyes after discovering that the woman he is married to is, in fact, his mother. In the tradition of the Jewish folktale, rabbinic literature offers us the legend of R. Matya b. Ḥeresh, who drove nails into his eyes so as not to be tempted by the image of a woman that was revealed to him and would have prevented him from studying Torah.

R. Matya ben Ḥeresh, wealthy, God-fearing, and charitable, was a seeker of virtue, who enriched scholars with his wisdom, always had orphans and widows at his table, and was honest in every way. All his days, he studied Torah like Rabbi Meir, his teacher, and his light radiated like the glow of the Sun. It was said of him that he never gazed upon any woman. Once he was sitting and studying Torah, and Satan passed by and envied him. Said Satan: Can there be in the world a righteous man who has never sinned? He immediately ascended to the heavens and appeared before the Almighty and asked: "What is R. Matya b. Ḥeresh to You?" God answered: "He is a perfectly righteous man." Satan then said: "Let me test him," and God let him. Satan then went and found R. Matya b. Ḥeresh studying Torah. He took on the appearance of a woman more beautiful than any other. When the rabbi saw her, he turned away, so Satan went to the other side and faced him again. Once more, the rabbi turned his face away and, yet again, Satan faced him. When R. Matya saw that "she" was confronting him from all sides, he said to himself: "I'm afraid that the evil inclination will vanquish me." What did this righteous man do? He called to one of his students who served him and said: "My son, bring me fire and nails!" When the student brought them, R. Matya heated the nails in the fire and drove them into his own eyes. When Satan saw this, he became frightened and fell back. He ascended to the heavens and told the Almighty what had happened.

God, then, called the healing angel, Raphael, and commanded him: "Go heal the eyes of R. Matya b. Ḥeresh!" The angel Raphael went down and stood before R. Matya. The rabbi asked Raphael: "Who are you?" Raphael answered: "I am God's angel Raphael; the Almighty sent me to heal your eyes." R. Matya answered: "I do not want that. What's done is done." The angel Raphael returned to the Almighty and told Him: "This is what R. Matya b. Ḥeresh said to me." Then the Almighty commanded Raphael: "Go to him and say: 'From this day forward, fear not. I promise you that the evil inclination will not vanquish you in this matter all the days of your life'." When R. Matya heard that from the angel, he allowed himself to be healed.[3]

In Jewish legend, the act of blinding oneself is a way of contending with erotic temptation, so R. Matya b. Ḥeresh is portrayed as a paragon of self-restraint.[4] In the former tale of the chaste maiden, the act of gouging out the eyes exemplifies a silent rebellion against a powerful man, trying to have her against her will. She harms herself, making herself unattractive, to deter him, simultaneously reaffirming the cultural connection between the eyes and sexual desire. In line with Jean-Paul Sartre's concept of "the look" or "the gaze," the maiden's self-awareness regarding her beauty comes about because the suitor gazes at her; in other words, his very gaze evokes her self-awareness, when she feels seen by the other. The gaze of the ruler courting her is what shaped her frightening awareness of being a woman.[5]

As such, control over the gaze is perceived as a virtue, since looking precedes the act; the gaze is a sign of desire and controlling it is a measure of self-restraint. However, the man's gaze and the woman's gaze usually have completely different interpretations in the gender field in most cultures. More often than not, a man may look at a woman, though his gaze is often intrusive and violent, while a woman may not gaze directly at a man, lest she be considered a bold temptress. Thus, in the absence of words, temptation is actualized by the gaze, as acquiescence to temptation.

Myths and legends focus on the taboo of gazing because it is akin to trespassing, and many cultures ascribe considerable importance to what a person may or may not see. In Genesis, Lot's wife disobeys the injunction not to look back at the destruction of Sodom when she flees with Lot and their family. In Greek mythology, the reckless and childish Psyche ignores her lover Eros's order to never look at him and, by doing so, loses Eros and his love forever. Similarly, Orpheus, who was ordered not to look back during his escape with Eurydice from Hades, does not obey and loses Eurydice forever. And cunning Perseus forces the Gorgon Medusa (whose gaze turns anyone who looks at her to stone) to gaze at her own reflection, thus defeating her.

In the folktale of the virgin who gouged out her eyes, the abstract concept of sight is transferred to the eyes themselves, as the organs of sight. It is not the gaze as a concept, but rather the physical eyes themselves that the maiden gives to the ruler. At the beginning of the tale, the lustful ruler was an active gazer; at the end, he had become the owner of the gaze of the woman he desired. This emblemization of the gaze is literally her eyes. The reader's attention is suddenly and shockingly diverted from the man's gaze to the woman's eyes—thereby emphasizing the immorality of his demand that she have intercourse with him against her will. Ironically, she saves herself by metaphorically giving him what he wanted and demanded. This is an exemplum of a Jewish female martyr.

The Maiden Who Jumped Off the Roof

Another folktale found in *Ṣemaḥ ṣaddiq* in the chapter on intemperance.

> ONCE THERE WAS a certain woman who was most chaste and pious, more so than all other women. She was already of a marriageable age but did not want to marry. Finally, after a number of women spoke to her day after day about the pleasure and enjoyment of coitus, she decided to try it. She summoned a suitor who had been asking for her hand in marriage for some days and slept with him a few times. Afterwards, she began to feel disgust at the abomination she had committed and regret at losing her virginity for no reason, having received nothing in return. So, she went up to the roof, jumped off, and died.

This pious woman is convinced to engage in sexual relations with a suitor but regrets her actions and kills herself by jumping off the roof. Her curiosity about sexual relations and the pleasure they provide exact the terrible price to be exacted from every woman for sexual permissiveness. The culmination of her bad conduct is suicide, the loss of the very body that experienced fleeting, corporeal pleasures, upon realizing their pointlessness.

What exactly is it that troubles this woman and drives her to suicide? There is no mention of any resulting societal rejection or condemnation due to her licentious actions. Apparently it is the same dissonance between the moral injunctions and desire for physical pleasures that first led her to chastity and, ultimately, to suicide. This suggests that even marriage—the Jewish legal justification for sexual relations—would not have resolved the dissonance, and that her only recourse should have been permanent celibacy, complete abstinence. Moreover, it is difficult to ignore the fact that, although this tale appears in a *musar* book, the spirit of the embedded tale is remote from the Jewish approach, which sanctifies sexual relations within the context of marriage for the purpose of procreation. Here her own sexual promiscuity was the reason for her suicide. Both the author and the readers accept her extreme act of self-punishment. (Note that suicide is rare in Jewish literature, in general, and is traditionally considered sinful).

What is especially interesting in this tale is the way that the women around her encourage her to behave in an inappropriate, sinful way, that is, to engage in extramarital sex. This suggests that the male author and his male readers perceive feminine friendship as potentially harmful and unwanted. The aggressive suitor, as the representative of male society, is pictured as being within his rights, whereas the women are depicted as being lustful and having a bad influence. Indeed, the lustful suitor is neither punished nor reproved, nor is he considered accountable for the shame he caused. The final lesson conveyed by the tale is found in its nonfictional context, which discusses the damage caused by addiction to bodily pleasures and sex.

We find several legends in rabbinic literature with a similar motif, associated with issues of forced or problematic intimacy between men and women, among them the suicide of Miriam the Hasmonean (b. Talmud, *Baba Batra* 3b) and of Beruriah, the wife of Rabbi Meir (in Rashi's commentary on the b. Talmud, *'Avodah Zara* 18b).[6] One such rabbinic tale follows:

> **Once there was a** young woman whose father had a good friend who was a gentile, and the two men would eat and drink together and enjoy themselves. The friend said to the father: "Give your daughter to my son in marriage." The young woman kept silent about the matter until the day of the planned wedding, when she climbed up to the roof, jumped off, and died.[7]

This midrashic tale presents the young woman as being righteous *post factum*, because she was unwilling to sin against Judaism by marrying a non-Jew. Since she was powerless in the face of her father's decision, she clearly felt that her only remaining option was to throw herself off the roof. The text suggests that the marriage agreement was likely made while both the principals were drunk, further underscoring the young woman's helplessness and fear of attempting to resist. This trope in which suicide is the solution to marrying an undesirable or socially unacceptable man was quite popular in medieval Jewish literature; during this era, legends spread about Jewish girls being under threat of rape or forced to marry non-Jewish men. It has a lot in common with the tales about self-mutilating maidens, both suggesting that self-injury is better than a shameful or inappropriate sexual liaison.

Medea

The tale that follows provides an exemplum of the adaptation of a plot taken from Greek tragedy for use in a Hebrew *musar* text.[8] It clearly indicates that *musar* authors did not shy away from pagan culture as long as it did not contradict their own Jewish values. In the case of this particular tale, the *musar* author slightly altered the ending of the original tragedy to better fit the Jewish ethos. It is also found in *Ṣemaḥ ṣaddiq*, in the chapter on cruelty.

> THE ANCIENTS WROTE THAT a woman named Medea lusted after a certain man. She pursued him, taking her younger brother with her. She, then, murdered her brother and cut him up into pieces, which she cast all about as she walked so that, when her father came after her, he would find evidence of this brutal cruelty and be too shocked to continue chasing her, thus letting her escape him. After being united with the man for whom she had lusted, she lived with him for a time and gave him two sons. Her husband eventually fell in love with another woman and left her, after which Medea murdered both her sons and drank their blood, to spite her husband. Then, she wandered here and there around the world. Her end is unknown.

This is a horrific Greek myth, rife with revenge. The above text is a short summary (translated from the original Hebrew prose) of the long and convoluted plot, dramatized by Euripides as a tragedy in the fifth century BCE and retold by Ovid in the first century CE. In Euripides's version, after Medea helps her husband, Jason the Argonaut, steal her father's golden fleece, she murders her own brother as the couple escape together. Later they settle down and have two sons. Eventually, Jason leaves Medea for Princess Glauce. Medea, a cruel and homicidal woman, in a fit of insanity, murders their two sons and kills Jason's bride. Medea flees in a flying golden chariot and finds asylum with King Aegeus. Most of these details are, of course, not included in the minimalist Hebrew version, which seems like a brief synopsis of the classic Greek plot, in which the *musar* author tried to eliminate the alien, polytheistic motifs while preserving the nonsectarian elements of condemnable human behavior.

Medea is portrayed in the ancient tragedy as a wicked monster driven by pure evil, and she became a symbol of maternal cruelty. She is a diabolical woman who harms innocents and shows no mercy or compassion toward any of her victims, not even her own children.

In the Jewish folklore tradition of the Middle Ages, there is a related folktale about Lilith, purportedly the first wife of Adam and created together with him, although she does not appear in the biblical account (Gen. 1:27). The tale relates that Adam abandoned Lilith, replacing her with Eve, the second woman, whom God created from his rib (Gen. 2:21–22). Out of revenge, Lilith has since lain in wait for Adam's male descendants, seeking, to this day, to kill them. This mythical threat is the basis for the plethora of cultural materials and customs designed to protect Jewish male infants during the first eight days of their lives, from the time of their birth until their circumcision.[9] The Lilith character is actually a postbiblical incarnation of Lamia, the snake-like, child-eating she-monster who kidnapped and ate children as an act of vengeance against Zeus and his wife, Hera, for stealing the offspring from her affair with Zeus.[10] The image of Lamia associates women with wild animals, reflecting the bestial side of womanhood.

Raping the Daughter as Punishment

Modern readers may find the next folktale very distressing, and we can only imagine its impact on its premodern audiences. But then again, such stories are easily remembered and have the greatest impact on their readers. Bear in mind that the predominant authorship and readership of *musar* literature were male, so the violent incidents toward women were from the male perspective. Here is a Jewish folktale found in Kaidanover's *Qav ha-yashar*, chapter 8.

> **In the days of the Ramban,** there was a scholar who was so devoted to Torah study that he would not even go to sleep at night. Even when he was eating, he studied Torah; he even missed prayer services because he was always studying. The Ramban warned him: "When it is time to eat, you must only eat, and when it is time to sleep, you must sleep, and when it is time to pray, you must pray. If you do this, the Torah will guard your life, but if you fail in this, you will offend the Torah, and the Torah will avenge its offense, and you will be punished." But the scholar did not heed the Ramban's warning and continued in his misguided way. One day, that scholar had to go to the market and, when he returned home, he found a knight raping his daughter on the very desk where he studied Torah. After seeing this, the scholar grieved for many days. Then, the Ramban said to him: "Remember that I warned you to be careful not to miss your prayers. Our sages determined that every Jew must pray every day and recite: 'O Lord, keep me out of the clutches of the wicked' [Ps. 140:4]. But you did not listen to me, and so your daughter was harmed."

This story counters the halo of constant Torah study, an elitist undertaking that was practiced only by the most scholarly Jewish men, reaffirming the importance of habitual, daily prayer, which is incumbent on every Jewish man. Despite the fact that not everyone is capable of such intense Torah study, one might think that *musar* texts would encourage the readers to become Torah scholars themselves; however, this tale lauds common people, the average Jew—the mainstream, target audience of *musar* literature. Perhaps it was thought that ordinary Jews only concern themselves with minimal obligations, but according to this tale, they are actually the real believers. Regular, normative prayer embody conformity, community life, and modesty, whereas extreme, ascetic Torah study is a solitary occupation engaged in by individuals who choose to seclude themselves. In general, mainstream Judaism rejects both asceticism and fanaticism.

This *musar* tale censures this excessive lifestyle as being contrary to the *musar* spirit, which is meant to teach Jewish norms and discusses everything relevant to all Jews. In a way, this tale promotes Aristotle's "golden mean," taking the middle path, that is, practicing moderation, not being too strict or too devout, so as not to lose touch with reality. The aforementioned scholar, for example, was guilty not only of neglecting his prayers but also of neglecting his daughter. Her rape on his desk, where he sat when he studied at home, also connects his sin to his punishment. However, the most direct connection between his lack of prayer and his daughter's rape is that both are violations—the father's violation of the Torah, by his immoderate behavior, led to his daughter's violation. The grievousness of excessive Torah study is the same as not studying Torah at all. By studying so much, he neglected the prayers that protect one from evil, so evil came into his home. Here, the violation of the daughter's body is equivalent to the violation of her father's body.

In traditional societies, unwed daughters are taught to stay chaste and unsullied, so as not to besmirch their fathers' and families' honor. Any loss of virginity outside a Jewish marriage is considered a serious violation. But the tale does not concern itself with the daughter's victimization. The author's message targets the scholar-father and does not consider the daughter's point of view at all. As such, it is a *musar* tragedy about the father, and the daughter merely serves as a means to punish him. Again, this *musar* work was intended for a male readership. The father, the main character, sins and is duly punished. The frightening punishment affected the readers, who were taught the proper way to conduct their own lives, through fear of the consequences of neglecting their prayers. This rabbinic tale emphasizes the power of routine, daily prayer, a normative habitus among ordinary Jews, to protect the common believer. In the Jewish ethos, Torah study by brilliant scholars is an ideal way of life. But here Ramban's tale restores a realistic balance, by praising standard Jewish religious practice.

The Adulteress and the Giant Dog

"The Adulteress and the Giant Dog" is a folktale found in chapter 34 of Kaidanover's *Qav ha-yashar*, which deals with ten offenses that lead to excommunication and banning.[11] Relevant to this discussion are six of these offenses: profanity; wasteful emission of semen; disregarding rabbinical mandates, such as ritual handwashing; disrespecting Torah scholars; desecrating God's name; and succumbing to the will of the wicked. The tale is presented as giving an example of a shameless offense for which the punishment is not only excommunication and ostracism in this world but also the reincarnation of the offender's soul as a dog.[12] Kaidanover's brief introduction to the tale warns, "And if you say reincarnation as a dog is a light punishment, come and see what happens in the following tale, and look at the punishment that came upon a married woman, God protect us." The ethical commentary that follows the tale also reinforces the two prohibitions—shamelessness and adultery—and links them together: "Come and see how the wrongs of the shameless incur the penalty of reincarnation as a dog, like the wrongdoing of the married woman. Therefore, a human being must comport himself modestly and the fear of God should always be upon him; then life will be good for him."

A TALE APPEARS in the writings of the Holy Ari.[13] In his day, there was a certain pious man named R. Avraham ibn Po'ah. He was very wealthy and always provided for the poor and the needy. Another Jew lived nearby, who was involved in commerce with R. Avraham's wife, since she was a clever businesswoman. One day this neighbor suddenly took ill and was confined to his bed for many days. Gradually, his flesh began to rot away, including his reproductive organ. He spent enormous amounts of money on medical treatment but found no remedy for his ailment. He finally died after intense and bitter suffering. Several years later, a dog appeared and began circling R. Avraham's home. It was a very ugly black dog. Those who saw it were quite afraid, since its face was that of an evil spirit. Time after time, they chased the frightening dog away from R. Avraham's house with sticks, but it kept coming back. Whenever R. Avraham arose to go to the synagogue, he would find that black dog standing by the door, waiting for him to open it, whereupon it would try to force its way inside. R. Avraham would chase the dog away and then lock the door behind him. Nevertheless, the dog would return and wait once more for the door to be opened.

One morning when R. Avraham left the house, he forgot to lock the main entrance door, as well as one of the inner doors. Immediately, the dog sprang forward, running from room to room, until it found the one where R. Avraham's wife lay in bed, still asleep. The dog jumped up on the bed and began biting her, again and again, inflicting many wounds, and then it fled the house. The woman let out such a great cry that her voice was heard even in the house of the Holy Ari. R. Avraham, accompanied by other men of the community, went to the Holy Ari for counsel, who told them that the reason for the attack was the woman's many sins, that she had committed adultery with her neighbor who was now dead, and that this black dog was the reincarnation of his soul. She had seduced the man with words and with money and the dog had now come to take revenge upon her. On hearing this, the men made the woman take an oath to tell the truth, and she admitted that her neighbor had indeed slept with her in the storehouse. That was why his flesh, including that of his reproductive organ, had rotted away. The pious R. Avraham immediately banished her from his home. Afterwards, the woman sought to repent and died in the course of doing penance.

Dogs, wolves, lions, and other predators present in folktales about adultery and other kinds of forbidden sexual intercourse, as well as in tales reflecting an aversion to sexual intercourse, represent the male libido. Even in today's American slang, "bitch" as well as "son of a bitch" are profanities that imply sexual promiscuity or the bestiality inherent in humans.[14]

In North American and Siberian folklore, there is a tale about the "dog husband," who is a dog by day and a married man by night. The villagers shun the wife, because she had relations with a dog and the couple had produced "dog boys."[15] A European tale tells of a talking dog, who tells the husband about his wife's infidelities.[16] Furthermore, there are European folktales about dog-headed people that devour humans as punishment for their sins.[17]

The myth of Amor and Psyche, from the Latin narrative poem *Metamorphoses* (also called *The Golden Ass*) by the Roman author Apuleius (second century BCE), tells of a beautiful princess delivered into the hands of a monstrous dragon, who is actually a sensitive young man. He makes their relationship conditional on her never looking at him, but she breaks the agreement, loses her beloved, and spends years wandering in search of him. Psychologist Erich Neumann interpreted this myth as an allegory of the development of female identity from dependence to independence and from immaturity to sexual maturity.[18]

The twelfth-century French tale "Bisclavert" (The werewolf) by Marie De France tells of a werewolf who marries a woman; he leaves when she betrays his trust and then returns, attacks her, and bites off her nose.[19] This story is reminiscent of the later tale "La Belle et la Bête," originally written in 1740 by Madame Gabrielle-Suzanne de Villeneuve (ca. 1685–1755) and then rewritten by Jeanne-Marie Leprince de Beaumont (1711–1780). In this tale, a spell is cast upon a young prince that turns him into a menacing monster, but a kiss from his beloved breaks the spell.

All of these plots echo a sexual relationship between a woman and a wild beast, a beast that is, in fact, a man under a spell. In Christian myths and stories, the spell is witchcraft, whereas in Jewish tales, it is a specific punishment for adultery. Psychoanalysts such as Bruno Bettelheim interpreted these stories as expressing the anxiety of young brides regarding intercourse on their wedding nights, when their husbands are mature, experienced men. The mysterious Gothic tone of these stories, along with their sexual connotations, are what make them attractive. The common cultural anxiety represented by such metaphorical dogs and other predators is the libidinous one of an uncontrollable sexual urge. This dog is, in fact, mankind.

The problem with "The Adulteress and the Giant Dog" is that it implies several different punishments for the sin of adultery, and it is unclear which of them is the most severe and who is actually being punished. The neighbor was punished in three ways: venereal disease, premature death, and reincarnation as a wild dog. The woman was punished with three penalties: assault by a wild dog, divorce, and death. A typical reader might still ask: Who is the real sinner? Is it the woman, the neighbor, or both? Who was the worst sinner and got the most severe punishment?

The punishments described in *Qav ha-yashar* raise questions, because they do not correlate with what Kaidanover wrote in the prologue and epilogue. According to the prologue, anyone who acts shamelessly or brazenly is reincarnated as a dog. Here, it is necessary to explain that "brazenness" is a euphemism for adultery. According to the epilogue, reincarnation as a dog is the punishment for adultery, so it is unclear why only the neighbor was punished in this way and not the adulterous wife, as well. It seems as though the man is being punished, but not the woman, although she is the one bitten, forced to leave her home and her marriage, and also dies prematurely. Furthermore, all of these punishments are physical penalties that carry sexual connotations: the disease that attacks the man's private parts, his reincarnation as a wild animal, and the assault on the adulterous wife in her bed. These forms of punishment highlight the sexual aspect of the situation and reveal the characters' sexuality to the readership. If we compare the punishment described in *Qav ha-yashar* with those described in other ethical works, we find that a dog's bite, as punishment for a sexual transgression, is a familiar motif in both Jewish and Christian folklore traditions. For example, in R. Elijah's *Shēveṭ Musar*, we read:

> When desire comes to incite you to commit an offense, immediately imagine the image of a great man, whom you know and fear as if he were in front of you, actually sitting on the Chair of Judgment with an angry countenance and full of wrath against you. Let your mind settle on that imagery and this should frighten you, as if it were in fact true and that great man was really standing before you. With this vision, the desire will weaken, because what kind of person sees such a great man in front of him and is still aroused to transgress before him, especially before a personage of whom he is in awe? Then, continue

> to contemplate and imagine in your mind's eye that you are standing in the presence of the *Shekhinah* [the Divine Presence], whose glory fills the entire world, and terror and fear will strike you and subdue your unruly heart. And if, even now, your desire has not been subjugated, when next confronted by the thought of transgressing, imagine that wild dogs are howling, and evil beasts are devouring people and ripping human flesh with their teeth.

In contrast to the explicit narrative in *Qav ha-yashar*, the wording of *Shēveṭ Musar* does not specify where, when, and on what occasion one will be bitten, thus arousing fear, while obscuring the physical details of the punisher and the punishment. Moreover, in *Shēveṭ Musar*, the discussion is on a theoretical level—a general ethical sermon—whereas *Qav ha-yashar* offers a visceral, illustrative tale. A folktale, by its very nature, is more personal and more specific and, no doubt, serves as a more effective deterrent.

An earlier example of a situation in which adulterers were attacked by a beast appears in a Jewish narrative about R. Meir, which recounts that during a journey to Jerusalem, R. Meir sinned by committing adultery with his host's wife.[20] In this case, a lion is sent by God to punish the sinner.[21] In this folktale, the creature's conduct indicates the truth about innocence or guilt. The following is a brief version.

> RABBI MEIR USED TO MAKE an annual pilgrimage to Jerusalem, where he was hosted by his friend Yehudah, the butcher, and his wife. The wife treated their guest with great respect. Once, R. Meir arrived at the house and found another woman there. He was told that the first wife had died and that the butcher had remarried. R. Meir was very saddened. Yehudah gave instructions to his new wife on how to treat their guest, but in her husband's absence, she plied him with wine until he was drunk and then seduced him. In the morning R. Meir awakened, ate breakfast, and wondered why his friend's wife was being overly intimate toward him. The woman told him that he had spent the night with her and that there was no need to be embarrassed; she even mentioned certain marks on

> parts of his body, as proof of what had happened. Upon hearing this, R. Meir left Yehudah's house in haste and went to the Head Rabbi of the yeshiva, where he recounted all that had transpired. Then, R. Meir asked the Head Rabbi to use the full force of Jewish law to punish him. After consulting with his scholarly peers, the Head Rabbi decided that, in order for R. Meir to atone for his actions, he must be left in the forest as prey for the lions. R. Meir accepted this verdict and was brought to the forest and left bound. Nevertheless, over the course of two nights, no lion harmed him. On the third night, a lion came and bit him near his ribs but left him alive. When the Head Rabbi saw this, he ruled that R. Meir had atoned for his sin and was allowed to return home. Some versions say that a heavenly voice announced that R. Meir was blameless.

In Thompson's *Motif Index of Folk Literature*, motif B522.3, we read about a woman accused of adultery who is cast into a lion's den, but the lion does not harm her. This theme is the closest, in spirit, to that of the Jewish tale; however, in that European folktale, the protagonist was an innocent woman who was unable to prevent a libelous story being told about her. There is an entire section about the tests of truthfulness (H200–299) in Thompson's *Motif Index*, and among these H210 is labeled as being a "test of guilt or innocence."[22] Tubach's *Index Exemplorum* distinguishes two story types, characteristic of the medieval religious tale, and both link adultery to punishment by lions.[23] An example of the first type is found in tale no. 58—about a woman suspected of adultery, who was thrown into a lion's pit as punishment, but the lion did not touch her, proving her innocence. The second type of tale is found in no. 3061, which describes a hermit besotted with desire. To punish himself, he leaves his hut and goes to lie down at the entrance to a lion's den, but instead of attacking, the lion licks him. Motif *Q557.4 of the Rotunda *Motif Index* similarly speaks of lions that do not harm the innocent thrown to them for punishment, particularly women suspected of adultery.[24]

Some of these folktales have historical documentation. The incident known as "La Bête du Gévaudan," which gained notoriety in 1764, concerns a fierce man-eating beast that terrorized the province of Gévaudan, killing people by tearing out their throats and then devouring them. The king of France invested large sums of money to deploy a huge number of soldiers, policemen, and hunters to hunt down the wild beast. Whether many stories developed from this specific case, sometimes historical events do find their way into folktales. As Robert Darnton noted, people tend to think more about specific events than about theoretical assumptions, and folktales help them make sense of the world.[25]

The tale of "The Adulteress and the Giant Dog" is a tragedy told from the male perspective, but actually accentuates the poor treatment of the woman. This explains why we may think that both the sin and the punishment belong to the neighbor, who engaged in adultery with a married woman and was severely punished by being reincarnated as a wild beast. This tale also raises the question about a world without redemption.

The Evil Neighbor

The final story (by an anonymous author) exemplifying *musar* tragedy, which tells of a sinner who violates all Ten Commandments, one after another, is found in the chapter on jealousy in *Orḥot Ṣaddiqim*. As in the previous tale, this one also refers to a situation in which a strange man comes between a married couple. As in the tale "Raping the Daughter as Punishment," here too, the tale refers directly to one of the daily morning prayers, "*Yehi Raṣon*," which reads, "May it be Your will . . . my God . . . to protect me . . . from evil neighbors."[26]

> ONCE, THERE WAS A MAN WHO had an evil neighbor, who coveted his wife and his property. There was one wall between his house and the neighbor's house. One day, from the other side of the wall, the neighbor heard the husband, a merchant, telling his wife that he had to travel for business and was leaving. What did the evil neighbor do after the husband had gone? On Friday night, he broke down the wall between the two houses, ignoring "Remember the Sabbath day." Then, he raped the man's wife, brazenly breaking the commandments "Thou shalt not covet" and "Thou shalt not commit adultery." He proceeded to steal her husband's money,

> disregarding "Thou shalt not steal," and when the wife began to scream, he murdered her, committing "Thou shalt not murder."
>
> When his parents admonished him, he struck them, defying "Honor thy father and thy mother." Even when he was brought before the Jewish court, he took an evil friend with him, who testified that the merchant-husband's property was mortgaged to him and that thieves had broken the wall and killed the wife, defying the commandment "Thou shalt not bear false witness against thy neighbor." And everywhere he went, he swore that he was innocent, thus breaking the commandment "Thou shalt not take the name of God in vain." Eventually all his evil was revealed, and all his crimes were discovered, and he was so ashamed that he lost his faith in God, violating "Thou shalt have no other God before me." Ultimately, he became a worshiper of idols, violating "Thou shalt not make unto thee any graven image." And all this was due to covetousness.

This tale is a brief, practical guide, warning the readers how quickly and easily the Ten Commandments might be broken by anyone fallen into evildoing. Especially note that the two distinct clusters of Ten Commandments appear in reverse in this tale, compared to their original, biblical order. Rather than beginning with those commandments dealing with the relationship between humanity and God and ending with those to be observed by Jewish society, this tale illustrates how covetousness and adultery may ultimately culminate in the loss of one's faith. The unknown *musar* author implies that giving in to one's unchecked urges is a most dangerous thing and leads to one sin after another. Again, setting aside the common, male-oriented gender issue (the exploitation of the female body to make a point), the *musar* message being promoted here is that even indulging a relatively minor sin (such as secretly longing for a married woman) can lead to the biggest sin of all—the renunciation of God. Of course, today's modern readers notice that, in these premodern tales, rape was not considered as terrible and serious a sin as it is perceived today. The instrumental attitude toward women's bodies, using women's bodies to punish men (also found in "Raping the Daughter as Punishment") is a consistent theme.

Figure 6. Kad ha-Qemaḥ, Sudylkiv 1837, title page. Courtesy of the Rare Book Collection at Bar-Ilan University.

To conclude this chapter, the *musar* tragedy is a tale strategically embedded in a *musar* work, amid its didactic, nonfiction prose. The strange and exciting plots of these *musar* tragedies not only punish the protagonists for their terrible sins (as expected and appreciated by the readership), but also describe horrible incidents that provide exposure to human transgressions, most of all by attempting to etch the fear of God and terrible divine punishment into the minds of the readers.

3

THE *MUSAR* COMEDY TALE

Can comedy and morality go together? Just like the tragedy, the moral comedy wants to warn the readers about wrong behavior, but it does it with a different poetic move. There is a blurry line between tragedy and comedy, and the authors of ethical books walk it carefully.

This chapter presents a select, exemplary group of *musar* comedies chosen from those existing in the corpus gathered for this research, along with explanations of why they should be considered ethical comedies. The comedy genre appears in a very significant number of *musar* texts, and it is especially important, since it marks the path to redemption, by showing readers how to acquire virtues and how to behave properly. The comedic protagonists serve as positive role models for the readers. When applying hermeneutic and inductive analyses to this genre, it becomes evident that the carnivalesque element plays a central role.[1]

The argument that follows is based on two stipulations. The first is that all the exemplary *musar* tales under discussion in this book come from the prepared research corpus, collected from Hebrew *musar* literature printed during the premodern and early modern eras, tales never before considered from literary structural and folkloristic perspectives, nor previously categorized as ethical comedies. Also note that the chosen tales are presented without their epilogues or prologues and are unaccompanied by the nonfictional *musar* texts in which they were originally embedded; as such, the present focus is exclusively on these tales and their internal literary features.[2] Furthermore, no formal definition of comedy has been adopted at the outset, so that a novel, inductively derived definition can be arrived at. Thus the second stipulation is a working definition of comedy formulated for this study: comedies end well for the main characters and in the minds of the readers. Though some of the more familiar tales may have other versions elsewhere, the selected comedies are studied as part of a distinct group of *musar* genre tales.

The following *musar* comedies are remarkably diverse, having a wide range of plots (i.e., plots, such as "the fisherman and his wife" or "the princess and the frog") and a broad spectrum of literary subjects (e.g., from greed to matchmaking). They all imply that divine grace is infinite and may be revealed in many different ways; there is much good in the world and God's blessings may be shared by everyone deserving of them.

What, then, are the common denominators that make all of these *musar* comedies? On what grounds may they be included in the same genre? Although comedy has a long tradition, dating from ancient Greece, this study treats it only in its social context, and not as jokes meant to elicit laughter. In other words, these *musar* comedies are certainly not jokes and were not meant to cause laughter and amusement, but rather to encourage the reader to rethink his or her life and conduct by revealing paths that can lead to well-being and success. As such, the Jewish *musar* comedy is quite different from ancient, medieval, and Renaissance comedies, in that it was not meant to entertain, but was intentionally designed and embedded to be didactic.

Comedy provides a different perspective, a way of thinking about life that serves as an effective, instructive medium in the *musar* literature. The meaning of the word evolved over the years. In Greek, *komoidia* meant "a mocking song." In classical culture, comedy and tragedy were the two basic types of drama, both of which may have developed from the Dionysian rituals. However, in contrast to tragedy, comedy was characterized by a simple, plebeian protagonist, meant to entertain the crowds. The first comedic characters and themes focused on political or social issues inspired by everyday life. Since the comedies featured amusing tones and nonelitist themes, they were perceived as a less important and less dignified art form. There are three types of comedy: (1) the character comedy, in which the protagonists reveal the weaknesses of human characters; (2) the social comedy, which exposes the weaknesses of a social group or a historical period; and (3) the practical joke comedy, which is based on antics and hoaxes. But these distinctions are not strictly adhered to and often these types intermingle.[3]

The classical Greek comedies (those of Aristophanes, Menander, and others) and Roman ones (by Titus Maccius Plautus and Publius Terentius Afer) influenced the Renaissance drama of Italy, France, Spain, and England. Shakespeare introduced fantasy into his comedies, Molière wrote character comedies, and Pierre Beaumarchais (1732–99) developed comedies that featured a political or social direction. In Italy, groups of the Commedia dell'arte staged performances characterized by improvisation and pantomime, using such stock characters as the fool, the doctor, and the miserly man.[4]

Ancient Greek comedy is usually divided into three periods: Old Comedy (*Archaia*, 446 BCE), Middle Comedy (*Mese*, 408–332 BCE), and New Comedy (*Nea*, 332–260 BCE). Theorists of ancient comedy hold differing views regarding the structure of the plays and their connection to Dionysian rituals. Gilbert Murray's model of the tragedy features six parts of the classical comedy: *agon* (conflict), *pathos* (passion), *threnos* (lamentation), *anagnorisis* (resurrection), and epiphany (celebration), whereas Francis Macdonald Cornford's model of comedy includes *agon*, *parabasis* (addressing the audience), sacrifice,[5] feast, marriage,[6] and *komos* (the drinking ritual)—with only *agon*, the contest between the old-year spirit and the new one, figuring in both models. In Rozik's characterization of the two, the principal theme of the comedy according to Murray is "divine death and resurrection," whereas that of Cornford's sequence is the "vegetational fertility" of nature. Cornford's view is based on later comedies, which, according to his interpretation, illustrated the uniting of nature or the metaphorical "marriage of Heaven and Earth." Rozik's diachronic reading of comedies shows, he claims, that the happy ending, which is now alleged to be a necessary component of comedies, is something that was only introduced in later years.[7] Both of those readings demonstrate the flexible nature of premodern drama and the shifts in the term "comedy," in particular the distinction between the popular use of the word today and its use in ancient cultures.

Myth-criticism argues that comedy had its origins in spring rituals, which is the reason it emphasizes a societal and collective approach to dilemmas and conflicts. Comedy, like tragedy, has always had implications for collective life, invoking an unleashed carnival spirit, thus attempting to expose the repressive powers of society. As such, comedies feature scapegoats, whose ultimate repudiation allows for an overhaul of traditional social values. According to Northrop Frye, Renaissance comedy, with its novel plots—which featured romantic situations and attempts by parents to foil them, placing the comedic conflict within the family and focusing on family matters—formed the foundation for premodern and modern comedy.[8]

Only the literary definitions, based on modern developments in this genre, align "comedy" with comic amusement and laughter. As Peter Childs and Roger Fowler contend, the tendency is to derive delight from watching characters who come to find certain situations difficult and problematical, while to the audience they are clear and simple.[9] A frequent side-effect of the enhanced empathy of the readership (or audience) with the comic protagonists may be the dissociation of a comedy from moral issues; in other words, some comedies may have moral messages while others may not, also affecting the comedic language, which cannot be too sophisticated or pretentious.[10]

The application of the comedy genre to *musar* literature proposes a new way of looking at a subset of *musar* tales as a way of thinking about Jewish life and about the relationship between human beings and God. This chapter studies several tales found in *musar* works and argues that they are Jewish *musar* comedies. The present model is supported by an inductive process and is the outcome of an in-depth study of the entire corpus of collected *musar* tales, as categorized in accordance with their specific plot features and the characteristics of their protagonists. Here, the following formula for the study of *musar* comedy is applied. From a structural perspective, the plot moves from a low point to a high one in regard to the state of the main character, which means that the story describes progressive personal growth, associated with the welfare and happiness of that character. From the perspective of the social context, as far as the protagonist is concerned, the story has a happy ending, consistent with the ethos of Jewish culture. As such, the *musar* comedies' conclusions reaffirm the values of Jewish society, with the main character representing the positive values espoused by the Jewish ethos. Moreover, it is by abiding by Jewish ethical values that the protagonist wins his or her reward in life or in the afterlife.

By means of the abovementioned formula for identifying comedies, table 2 outlines their common scheme, based on the plots' divisibility into three parts: the first episode (sometimes called the exposition), the middle episode, and the third and final episode.

The first tale discussed in this chapter has one of the most radical plots in the whole collection, because it stretches gender distinctions and describes a special miracle. It supports the idea that the *musar* authors were far more concerned with the didactic messages found in these embedded tales than with the outlandish nature of their plots. This particular tale also proves that *musar* tales may be very short, yet still serve a complete comedic function, moving quickly from the introduction of the

Table 2. The *Musar* Comedy

Plot structure	**First episode**	**Second episode**	**Final episode**
Main character in action	Problem: The protagonist is being tested.	Test: The protagonist successfully passes the test.	Solution: The protagonist is duly rewarded.
Main character's welfare	Reaches the lowest point.	Displays personal growth and progress.	Reaches the highest point.
Main character as a model	Reaffirms Jewish values.	Reaffirms Jewish social norms.	Reaffirms collective, traditional values.
Telos	Consistent with Jewish ethos.	Consistent with Jewish ethos.	Consistent with Jewish ethos.

issue, through the conflict, and reaching a good resolution at the end; that is, it includes the full complement of a comedic plot.[11]

The Father Who Breastfed His Son

This provocative tale is found in the prologue of R. Aboab's *Menorat ha-Ma'or*, in the context of a discussion on the sin of envy.

> THERE WAS A MAN WHOSE wife died, and she left him with his newborn baby boy, who was still nursing. This man had no money to pay for a wet nurse. Miraculously, his breasts were transformed into female breasts, so he was himself able to suckle his son.

An earlier version of this tale may be found in the Babylonian Talmud, *Shabbat* 53a. Here it appears in the context of the bad consequences of envy, for it explains the idea that, when a person is content with what he has and does not become envious over what others have, then he is rewarded. Clearly, this aforementioned widower is very poor and cannot afford to hire a wet nurse. Since he does not complain about his hard lot, God sees his misery and helps him. This tale has a positive ending, since the protagonist, the poor widower and father, goes from a very low point in his life toward the solution to his problems. This miraculous resolution not only provides a means for feeding the baby but ensures the continuity of the family lineage, the baby boy being the next dynastic link. The importance of that baby's life is so great that God, the Omnipotent, alters the natural order, by partially transforming this man into a wet nurse.

This is not the only time that this motif appears in Jewish tradition. Another, earlier version of this rabbinic legend may be found in *Bereshit rabbah* 30:8, concerning Mordecai, who became Hadassah's foster father (in the biblical book of Esther), and breastfed her.[12] This Jewish motif originated in Greek and Roman mythology. Zeus was nurtured by Amalthea (sometimes represented as a goat) inside a cave in Cretan Mount Aigaion (Goat Mountain),[13] and Romulus and Remus were suckled by a she-wolf.[14] These myths imply that individuals nurtured by animals are the "chosen ones"—those for whom nature was altered to keep them alive.

What makes the Jewish tale special is that it describes not only the violation of the laws of nature, but also of the "laws of gender."[15] The plot moves toward rewarding the main character for his piety, while also reflecting the fear of losing the newborn child and, by that, also losing dynastic continuity. This anxiety about becoming extinct is one of the most dominant subjects in Jewish literature, and is expressed in a wide range of literary motifs. "The Father Who Breastfed His Son" reflects an extreme manifestation of that ever-present, collective Jewish fear.

This very strange tale is apparently unique, since the research did not locate any other versions of it anywhere in the *musar* literature. However, the legend of Magdalena Ventura, rendered in paint by the Tenebrist painter Jusepe de Ribera in Naples around 1631, is reminiscent. The painting shows Magdalena, who looks like a manly, bearded figure, breastfeeding a baby, with her sexuality undoubtedly being tested, since her husband is standing close behind her; the two look like a homosexual couple. Actually, this pair of two bearded men, one of them breastfeeding a baby, may have appeared monstrous; perhaps the painting had the effect of the popular oral folktales about giant dogs (and other hairy beasts) that were circulating in the general population. The Jewish themes in the *musar* tale may depend on its being embedded in a *musar* work.

In contrast, the next tale begins with the death of a father and his last will, and the plot deals with three generations: the father, the son, and the grandson, once again illustrating the typical Jewish concern regarding the continuity of the generations. The plot includes a puzzling twist.

The Loyal Sons

This tale is found in Judah the Pious's late twelfth to early thirteenth-century compilation, *Sefer Ḥasidim*, no. 166.

> **Once upon a time** there was a son who honored his father greatly. His father told him: "If you honor me so much when I am alive, please continue to honor me after my death. I command you to always restrain your anger for one night." After his father died, the son went traveling overseas, leaving his wife behind and, although he did

not know it, she was pregnant. He was gone for many years. Then, unexpectedly, he returned home. He arrived home at night and went straight up to his wife's bedroom, where he knew she used to sleep. Suddenly, he heard a young man kissing her in her bedroom. The husband pulled out his sword to kill them both, but he remembered his father's command and sheathed the sword. Then he heard his wife say to the young man: "You should marry already. I wish your father knew that and would come home to give you away." When the husband heard this, he said: "Open the door to me . . . my love. Blessed be God and blessed be my father for causing me to hold back my anger and for not killing you and my son." And they made a feast for all the Jews and were very happy and joyful.

First, it should be noted that the compiler of *Sefer Ḥasidim* did not invent this tale. It is, in fact, a very old and well-known one, found in both Jewish and non-Jewish European traditions. As is common of international folktales, this one accompanies two thematically different *musar* lessons. In the first, as in *Sefer Ḥasidim*, it is used to illustrate the potential destructiveness of unchecked anger. Many *musar* works, from those of R. Sa'adia Ga'on in the tenth century to R. Elijah ha-Kohen's eighteenth-century work *Shēveṭ Musar*, devote lengthy discussions to denouncing anger. Hence, this discussion in *Sefer Ḥasidim* is not unusual. The second lesson derived from the plot is to always heed the wise man or elder, even if the advice seems puzzling or illogical, because it will, ultimately, prove to be right. It seems likely that the compiler was influenced by the following rabbinic legend, found in the Babylonian Talmud, *Ketubot* 62b, which is similar, but develops the plot in a different direction.

Rabbi Ḥama Bar Bissa left his home for twelve years to study Torah. When he returned, first he went to the local synagogue. At the same time his son, Rabbi Hoshaya, who was now a grown man, came into the synagogue, but Rabbi Ḥama did not recognize him. His son was brilliant and was noted for saying wise things, and the two men had a scholarly conversation. Rabbi Ḥama listened to him and was upset. He said to himself: "If only I had a son like him." He

> then returned home, looking for his wife, whom he had not seen for twelve years. Meanwhile, his son also entered in the house. Rabbi Ḥama wondered: "What is he doing here? Did he follow me to continue our conversation?" Rabbi Ḥama felt so honored that he stood up before Rabbi Hoshaya. Then, his wife said to him: "A father does not have to stand up when his son enters the house."

The internal structure of these plots is similar: a father who returns home after a long absence does not recognize the man in the house as his son. The talmudic tale, however, does not suggest any sort of marital betrayal or disloyalty. Moreover, it is not presented in a *musar* context, but rather within the general framework of the daily experience of Jewish scholars, struggling with the dual challenge of pursuing Torah study while maintaining good family life. The purpose of this talmudic story, as shown by its place in the tractate, was to discuss the price paid by scholars and their families, when the former choose to devote themselves to the study of Torah. True, they father children, but their sons grow up as orphans. True, they may become famous, but they are eventually estranged from families and homes.

Although this discussion is focused on Jewish literature, one cannot ignore a similar and relevant story told in Homer's *Odyssey*, written in the eighth century BCE.[16] Odysseus is the classic prototype of the hero in the Western adventure story. He returns to Ithaca after ten years' absence, during which he had served Calypso and had many adventures in the lands around the Aegean Sea. Upon his return, he first becomes acquainted with his son, Telemachus, who was already a grown man and independent. Together, they murder all of Penelope's suitors, who were staying in Odysseus's home and behaving as though it was their own. The commonality between the story of Odysseus and the folktale embedded in *Sefer Ḥasidim* is that, in both cases, the husband embarks on a long journey and is away for a very long time. Furthermore, they both raise the question of the woman's loyalty to her absent husband and, finally, the husband meets his adult son upon his return.

Sefer Ḥasidim reflects three prior literary influences: Homeric myth, adventure literature, and, of course, rabbinic legends. But whereas the purpose of a *musar* tale is to encourage the reader to sustain personal and group conformity, that is, to eliminate any trace of individualism, the adventure story has a diametrically opposed message. The hero of an adventure story is an individualist—a trailblazer, a risk-taker, what people in the twenty-first century would call "an adrenaline junkie." The adventurer is characterized by the ability to break through the time and space in which he was born and to leave the conformist world. An adventure story has a daring plot and the hero of such a story is a protagonist whose courage is his dominant characteristic.

In contrast, the hero of the *musar* tale must represent the values of the normative Jew. The *musar* author must always bring the Jewish hero back into the fold, even if the latter has left it at the outset. In other words, the teleology of *musar* literature is one of conformity.[17] Hence, if an adventure takes place within a *musar* tale, it must fail, so that the hero (and the reader) can learn a lesson from that failure. Thus the Jewish approach toward adventure in a *musar* work is ambivalent. In general, although there are adventures, they do not end well—and the Jewish hero always experiences some type of enlightenment that returns him to conformity, to normative Jewish behavior. Since Jewish social norms favor moderation and survival, so models of heroes, who intentionally court danger, are inconsistent with the Jewish ethos.

In fact, *musar* works are particularly conservative, designed not only to model proper conduct, but also to ensure that Jews do not leave safe spaces. What space did the ethos consider dangerous? What is a safe place for Jews? This answer may be found in a range of Jewish sources: Gen. 25:27: "And Esau was a cunning hunter, a man of the field, while Jacob was a quiet man, dwelling in tents"; Ps. 74:5: "Happy are they that dwell in Thy house"; *Mishnah Avot* 3:4: "He who walks alone forfeits his life"; j. Talmud *Shabbat* 2: "Rabbi Levi said: 'Satan is found in three places to lodge accusations against human beings: he who walks alone on the road, he who sleeps in a dark house alone, and he who sets sail on the great sea'"; Rashi's commentary on b. Talmud *Pesaḥim* 2a: "The best way to conduct oneself—He who sets out on the road will enter the inn in the evening, while the sun is still shining, and the next day, he will wait until the sun rises and then he will leave, and that way it is good for him, because the light is good for him. As it is written about the light [Gen. 1:4], that it is good. And what is it good for? Against wild animals and against robbers."

From the Bible to rabbinic and exegetic literature, Jewish sages all warned Jews against "the road"; they dealt with Jewish anxiety about leaving safe spaces: the home, the synagogue, and the Jewish community. All the above quotations are actually "silent" testimonies, textual oddments, residual memories of historic incidents that happened to Jews who left safety behind—a collective, traumatic memory of sorts, silent because they were undocumented historical memoirs, lacking actual details about specific individuals, lingering as general, cautionary folktales.

The authors of premodern *musar* literature were determined to keep Jews within safe space in order to protect their very lives—and not just Jewish values. For a Jew, time spent on the road was time spent unprotected, as such, an undesirable situation to be avoided as much as possible. Of course, those fears had historical bases, since Jews traveling in unfamiliar places were endangered by robbers and antisemitic pogroms. In general, adventure stories describe journeys taken by choice, sometimes out of opportunism—stemming from the adventurer's wish to be tested in difficult and dangerous situations, whereas the socio-historical reality of the Jew, as a member of an ethnic minority within a hostile majority, led to a Jewish attitude very suspicious of the urge for adventure. In fact, all the adventure tales included in the *musar* literature ultimately teach just this: "There's no place like home."

It seems that the anxiety conveyed by this tale in *Sefer Ḥasidim*, warning the readers to avoid all kinds of personal disasters, does not come solely or even primarily from the desire to dissuade people from committing murder due to excessive anger. It is also not particularly about universal moral values. Rather, it is a book written *by* Jews and specifically intended *for* Jewish readers, thus prioritizing intracultural values. The embedded tale expresses the fear of the potential loss of the next generation and the destruction of a Jewish family line, which is a common theme in Jewish folktales and probably is an outcome of Jewish communities being threatened by their surroundings throughout history. The husband's adventure might have caused him to kill his only son, jeopardizing his only contribution to the continued existence of his Jewish lineage. The moral of the tale is that Jews should only leave safe spaces out of necessity and not by choice, or on a whim. Thus adventure tales located in *musar* books have been diluted, because they do not present heroic protagonists, lauded for personal fame or personal gain. If there is an adventure, it is undertaken out of necessity, and its purpose is to teach some general moral lesson. Whereas the ethos of the Homeric myth glorifies personal heroism based on daring and resourcefulness in unexpected situations, the ethos of the *musar* comedy expresses the collective Jewish interest in avoiding danger insofar as possible.

The Jewish adventure tale also has reservations about glory achieved through physical heroism, so it does not deal with anything that happened to the hero when he was not at home. The crux of the plot is rather in the return home and in the family's reunion. The lesson taught by this tale in *Sefer Ḥasidim* is: Do not leave your home! Do not leave your wife and son! For if you do, there will not only be a disaster in the present, but it will destroy the entire future of your family.

Therefore, tale no. 166 concludes with a national celebration: "They made a feast for all the Jews." The adventurous son becomes a national hero, not merely for heeding the wisdom of his father, nor for restraining his anger and resheathing his sword, but for preserving the destiny of his own family, an irreplaceable part of the Jewish people. It is no coincidence that the narrator echoes the biblical book of Esther, the central theme of which is the salvation of the entire Jewish nation. Esther 2:5 begins a story about a Jew named Mordecai, who was the foster father of his beautiful, orphaned first cousin, named Hadassah (in Hebrew) or Esther (in Persian). Mordecai commands Esther (2:10) never to reveal her true ethnic identity, so that she may gain the king's favor and maintain her strategic position. Later on in the book, she is able to save the entire Jewish community from annihilation, thanks to her bravery and resourcefulness. The ability to establish and maintain Jewish communities was, in fact, the great adventure of the Jew in exile. Such *musar* comedies teach that the fate of the Jewish community is also the fate of the individual Jew and vice versa.

The next tale discusses a miraculous situation—a man encounters Elijah the Prophet and is granted his wishes. It adds an element of fantasy to

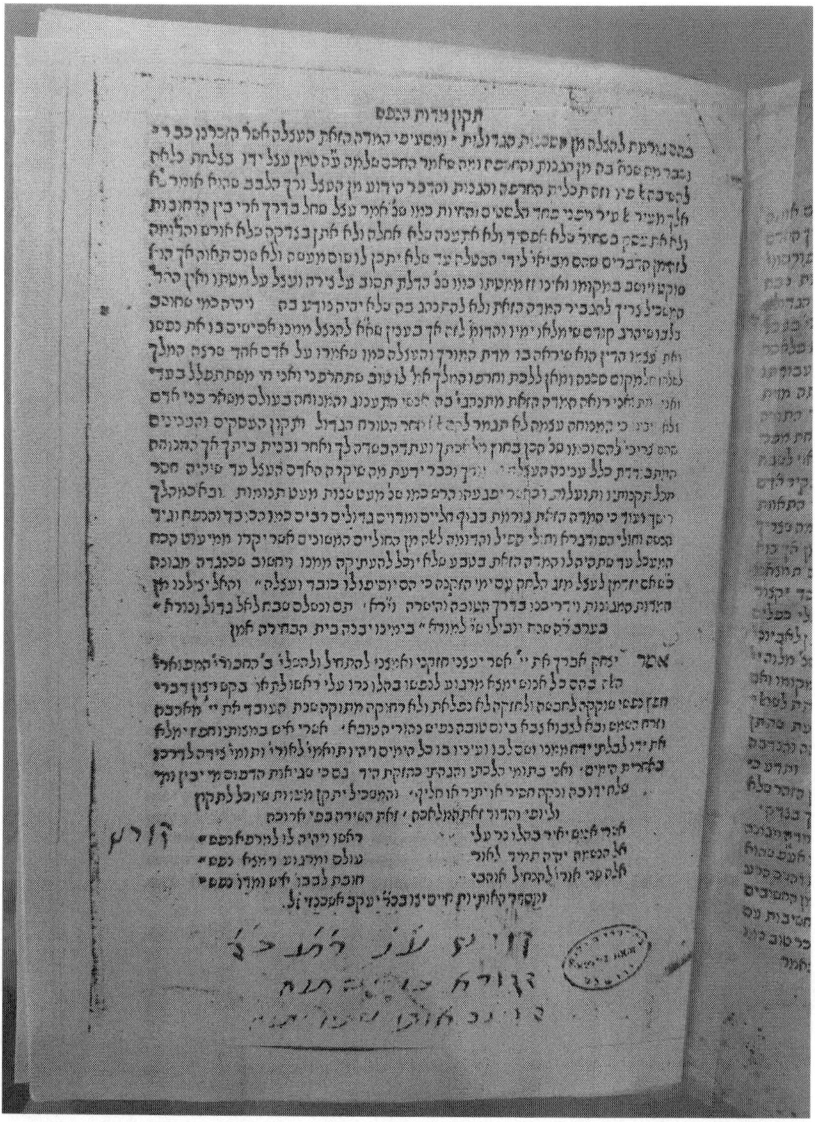
תקון מדות הנפש

Figure 7. Tiqun Middot ha-Nefesh, Constantinople 1550, epilogue. Courtesy of the Rare Book Collection at Bar-Ilan University.

the repertoire of motifs that appear in *musar* comedy tales, although *musar* comedies are, as we will see, sometimes realistic.

Six Good Years

The following tale, about the rewards of charity, is found in the first chapter of *Shēveṭ Musar* in the section that deals with rich people, who should give part of their wealth to the poor and to Torah scholars.

> **Once there was a pious man** with a righteous wife, who lost all his possessions, after which he had to work for wages to earn his living. One day, while he was plowing a field [in the Holy Land], he met Elijah the Prophet, disguised as an Arab, who told him: "I can give you six good years—when do you want to accept them, now or at the end of your life?" The pious man answered: "You must be a magician, for I have nothing to give you. Let me be!" But Elijah addressed him a second time and a third. On the third time, the pious man said: "I want to consult my wife." He went home to his wife and told her: "Someone came to me, bothered me three times, and suggested giving me six good years, saying that I can choose whether to receive them now or at the end of my life." And he asked her: "What do you say?" The wife told him: "Go and tell him: 'Bring them now!'" Then Elijah told the pious man: "Go to your home and the blessing will fall on your home even before you enter the gate of your yard." Meanwhile, the pious man's sons were digging in the yard, and they found a treasure that would support them very comfortably for six years, and they called their mother. When the pious man arrived at his garden gate, his wife ran out to him, immediately telling him the good news. He was joyful and expressed his gratitude to God.
>
> What did his wife do after this? She told her husband: "Since God, in his kindness, has given us good fortune for six years, we should give charity during those years; thus, we'll be rewarded." And so she did. Each day she said to her younger son: "Keep recording all our acts of kindness and charity!" And so he did. At the end of

> those six good years, Elijah the Prophet came back and said to the pious man: "Now it is time for me to take back everything I gave you!" But the pious man said: "When you first came, I consulted my wife, and now I want to consult her again." He went to his wife and told her: "Now that old man is here to take his grace with him." The wife answered: "Go and tell him that, if he finds someone more trustworthy than I, he can take it and give it to them." Then, God saw all their good works and rewarded them.

This tale is also found in *Rut Zuṭa* 4:11[18] and in *Yalquṭ Shim'oni*,[19] no. 607, regarding the Prophets and the Writings associated with the psalm "*Ēshet Ḥayil*" [A woman of valor] found in Prov. 31:10–31—which is not surprising, since, clearly, the wife is the key figure behind her husband's success.[20] This point is blurred in *Shēveṭ Musar*, which emphasizes the virtue of charity. The tale is a *musar* comedy, according to the criteria established in this study, since the husband and his wife begin in great poverty and, owing to their virtues, are saved by God. The principal theme is the commandment to practice charity. Many Jewish tales deal with the subject of charity, indirectly indicating the existence of distinct social classes in medieval Jewish society.

As for Elijah, the miraculous visitor, this motif appears quite frequently in Jewish folktales, beginning with the classic, rabbinic literature and continuing to this very day, as evidenced by many oral folktales collected in the Israel Folktale Archive (IFA). In contrast to his biblical image, postbiblical Elijah is the messenger of God tasked with helping pious people, sometimes appearing like an old man and sometimes otherwise disguised, a literary convention that is no surprise to the readers of *musar* literature.[21]

There are, however, two unusual elements that stand out in the plot of this particular tale. The first is that the wife tells the young son to record the charity she is giving—meaning that we are dealing with a literate society, in which even the children know how to read and write well. The second is the dominance of this wife, as the family's decision maker, placing her above her husband—although, as noted above, this issue is largely ignored by the context of charity in which the tale is embedded.[22]

Going beyond the fantastic nature of the previous tale, the next one employs a distinctive mythological atmosphere by introducing an angel, another iconic element of Jewish literature that serves as a component in *musar* comedy.

The Birth of Ishmael ben Elisha

This tale is found in chapter 24 of *Shēveṭ Musar*, which deals with the good conduct of a righteous woman.[23] It is embedded in a text dealing with the ritual immersion in a *mikveh* (a ritual bath) that every married Jewish woman must perform after her menstrual period, in order to restore her purity, so that she may resume sexual relations with her husband for the purpose of procreation. If this regular, monthly ritual (the wife's responsibility) was not done properly for any reason, it was thought that she could not conceive that month. The prologue of the tale notes that, if a woman encounters an impure animal after her immersion, she must return to the *mikveh* and repeat the ritual again, lest the newborn conceived resemble the impure animal she had seen.

> ELISHA, THE HIGH PRIEST, did not have sons. He prayed to God, saying: "Master of the whole world, why do all the righteous have sons and I do not?" Then God answered: "Because they strictly observe [Jewish] laws of purity before sexual intercourse." So Elisha went to his wife and taught her all the laws of purity, which they decided to follow meticulously. Then his wife went to the communal bath to undertake her ritual immersion but, each time she left the *mikveh*, she encountered an impure creature. First, she saw a leper, so she went back. Then she saw a camel and went back. On her sixth attempt, she encountered a dog, the seventh time—a horse, the ninth time—a moron, the tenth—a gentile—and each time she had to go back and immerse herself yet again.
>
> Then, God felt sorry for her and commanded the angel Metatron:[24] "This poor woman is suffering. Go and stand in front of her, so she can get home safely, conceive tonight, and give birth to a holy person!" Therefore, Metatron went down and sat on the threshold of

> the communal bath, but when she saw him as she was leaving, she started to go back inside. But he said: "You should know that I am the Angel Metatron, and God has sent me to you, since you have already suffered enough." His words made her very happy, and she went home, became pregnant, and bore R. Ishmael b. Elisha, who later became the High Priest. Baby Ishmael [whose name means "God heard"] was born beautiful. And their son was like Metatron, since Metatron was his godfather; whenever R. Ishmael wanted to go up to Heaven, he would mention the name that Metatron gave him, and he was allowed to ascend.[25]

This *musar* tale, which accounts for the beauty of newborn Ishmael, is related to other legends about Ishmael's beauty as an adult. It also explains why he could go up and down between Heaven and Earth. All these qualities, engendered by the miracles leading to his birth and his angel-like empowerment, are what made him a legendary figure, rather than an ordinary human being.[26] He is certainly not a typical hero. The folktale is framed as a biographical legend about the miraculous birth of a cultural hero. It talks about the prolonged infertility of the parents, the mother's longing to conceive the child, and the impact of the heavenly godfather on the baby's beauty and R. Ishmael's adult powers. It is not surprising that a heavenly creature comes to a woman who has a problem conceiving. This motif has many versions in connection with other biographical legends of cultural heroes (e.g., Samson, Jesus).[27]

Earlier written versions of this story may be found in medieval manuscripts, especially in a midrash known as *Ēlleh ezkerah*, devoted to the ten martyrs, among them R. Ishmael, who were executed by the Romans after the destruction of the Second Temple.[28]

However, as it is formulated in *Shēveṭ Musar*, and according to the subject of the chapter, the tale is supposed to focus on the behavior of the woman who gave birth to a healthy and a beautiful son, after conducting herself properly. As in "Six Good Years," it is clear that this wife has a major role in the plot and is regarded as taking responsibility for the domestic activities, the family's finances, and for helping the less fortunate in the Jewish community. Obviously, she is responsible for her pregnancy and the well-being of her baby, which suggests that the fate of the family line is in her hands. As in the tale of the nursing father, here too, the primary concern is the survival of the next generation.

The following *musar* tale is also a comedy, owing to a happy ending that prevails despite the misfortune of minor characters and the indeterminacy of its plot. Since it is not framed as a classic legend of reward, it raises many questions about the logic of life.

The Two Merchants and the Doomed Ship

This tale appears in the section on the virtue of joy in *Orḥot Ṣaddiqim.*

> Two merchants planned to sail away on a ship. But it happened that one of them was hurt when a thorn got stuck in his leg. The injured merchant could not travel, but his friend embarked, and the ship sailed. The injured merchant was very sad and cursed his ill luck, but after several days, he heard that the ship had sunk and that all the passengers that had been on it were dead. Then he began to praise God and understood that his injury was meant to save his life.

This tale is in a chapter that deals with gladness, designed to describe the value of joy and, especially, the virtue of being satisfied with what you have. It implies that one should even gladly accept miserable experiences in life, because one never knows what the ultimate benefit of ill fortune may be. An example of this is cited by the anonymous author of *Orḥot Ṣaddiqim* both in the prologue and in the epilogue to the tale: the legend of Naḥum Ish Gamzu, one of the symbols of suffering in rabbinic literature, whose physical discomfort and pain never prevented his constant gratitude to God.[29]

The tale of the two merchants is one of personal rescue, where the main character, the injured merchant, starts from a point of great disappointment, because his initial plans had been thwarted, but finally understands that the disruption saved him from disaster. Thus he finds himself in a very positive state at the end of the story, although he had not done anything to warrant his salvation; his salvation was divinely wrought, as was his injury. This tale supports the belief that everything that happens to a person is the will of God and that, ultimately, the good will of God is to do justice for each individual, even if humanity cannot always see God's grand scheme when untoward, unpleasant, or painful things occur. This view of life was influenced by medieval Islamic thought and found its way into some Jewish literary works.[30] An excellent example of a Jewish collection consisting of these kinds of tales is *Ḥibbur Yafeh meha-Yeshu'ah* by R. Nissim of Qairouan (a.k.a. Nissim Ga'on).[31] The book is based on the well-known folkloric motif, "For Want of a Nail," meaning that causality is a key to understanding failure and that very minor things in life may turn out to be crucial. While the European proverb, as reflected in medieval literary works in German, French, and English, refers to a sequence of failures, the Jewish tales describe movement toward joyful gratitude to God. Nonetheless, the main idea is the same in both.[32]

The final tale in this chapter on *musar* comedy takes the discussion from birth (the subject of the first example above) to death and the afterlife. It is a classic Jewish legend of reward, though it focuses on reward in the afterlife. The previous tales presented here confined themselves to the corporeal world, to rewards meted out during a person's lifetime, but this tale extends beyond the physical realm.

The Man with One Book

This tale is in Kaidanover's *Qav ha-yashar*, but there are earlier versions in Aboab's *Menorat ha-Ma'or* and in the Yiddish folklore anthology, *Mayseh Bukh*.[33]

COME AND SEE THE PIOUS MAN who lived in a small village. All he had was one volume of the talmudic tractate *Ḥagigah*, which he spent all his days reading. He lived for many years. At the end of his life, just before he passed away, that volume of *Ḥagigah* miraculously transformed into the figure of a woman, who walked before him after he died and led him to the afterlife, bringing him into Heaven.

In contrast to the prior comedies in this chapter, this tale describes rewards granted both during his lifetime (longevity) and in the afterlife (heavenly and physical pleasures). Nonetheless, it meets the criteria for comedy, as defined in this study, since the protagonist is rewarded for the virtuous conduct (devoutly studying the one tractate he had) he has exhibited throughout his long though poor and simple life (his test of endurance and commitment). Under the circumstances, he is entitled to a place in Heaven (his due reward). The conclusion makes his heavenly end far better than his meager existence. The implicit erotic hint in this brief tale (the figure of a woman) suggests that part of his heavenly reward, after his solitary existence, might include certain conjugal pleasures among the joys of Heaven, those that he had never experienced while alive. In diametric opposition, after having lived a long, impoverished, and celibate life, he did not die alone and his afterlife promises to compensate him spiritually, and sexually as well.[34]

No less unusual, this man had almost no books in his home, which is highly irregular in normative Jewish homes and quite contrary to the Jewish ethos. However, the tale talks about reading a book—not just any book, but a talmudic tractate, which implies either that he was so poor that he could not afford to buy more books or that he lived in such an isolated place that this was the only Hebrew book he could find. It suggests that even ordinary Jews kept printed books at home and engaged in reading and studying as a way of life. Moreover, studying rabbinic texts was not just something a Jew did when he happened to have some leisure time, but it was the essence of Jewish life.

The Babylonian Talmud has thirty-seven tractates, and *Ḥagigah* is one of the shortest and easiest of them. This implies, again, that the protagonist was exceedingly poor or barely educated, yet all his efforts were invested in maintaining a Jewish way of life, that is, learning *halakhah* (Jewish law, rules, and practices)—as much as possible. *Ḥagigah* has only twenty-six pages and is considered easy to learn. From this perspective, the tale implies that all the readers should try and do the same, to accept this protagonist as a role model, practicing a way of life that is possible for every Jewish man, regardless of his social status or level of education. However, the intimacy created between the reading protagonist and the text he repeatedly read was symbolized by the book's transformation into a woman. This tale makes it clear that, although the man was totally committed to his study, something was missing from his life. The missing element was a family, a wife and children, which are the earthly components of the heavenly ideal. His book becoming a woman demonstrates the understanding that God is all-seeing, watching every person, so everyone gets their just deserts, exactly what they need (comedy) or deserve (tragedy). The intimacy between the reader and the text was replaced by intimacy between a man and a woman. The book rewarded the pious man in a physical way.[35]

Of course, the tale's ultimate message is that Jews should do their best to study *halakhah* as much as they can and that, if they do so, they will enjoy longevity and reach Heaven in the afterlife. This *musar* comedy provides a happy ending both in this world and the next one.[36]

Although the six tales presented in this chapter do not share the same theme or plot, nor even teach the same virtues, they all adhere to the same metastructure, meeting the criteria that mark them as being Jewish comedies. They start at low points, at which the protagonists are tested in serious situations: one pious man is left to raise a newborn alone; a grieving son leaves his pregnant wife and his home for many years; another pious man loses his fortune and must work for wages; a High Priest is unable to beget sons; a merchant misses a boat due to an injury. Finally, a third pious man, a miserable, solitary bachelor, has only one book to read all his long, lonely life. These depictions (perhaps meant to serve as examples for the dominantly male readership) all reaffirm collective Jewish values: the widower prays for God's help and is miraculously transformed; the orphaned son abides by his father's will and is rewarded; the fortunate poor man who shares his good fortune with the needy ultimately gains greater fortune and longevity; the High Priest instructs his meticulous wife regarding purity before sexual relations, so God sends an angel to their aid, and they have an extraordinary son; the injured merchant learns to appreciate his lot and thanks God for saving him; and lastly, the solitary poor man, who reads the same talmudic tractate each and every day, is granted longevity, entry to Heaven, and compensation for his loneliness and abstinence.

These *musar* comedies deal with everyday Jewish life: parents and children, husbands and wives, wealth and poverty, marriage, livelihood, and leisure. They focus on Jewish conduct both in and out of the home. All these comedic characters (the Jewish "heroes") follow the desired Jewish way of life, pass their tests and trials successfully, and so are rewarded. These protagonists are humble, kind, and disciplined; they are usually family oriented and do not challenge Jewish social norms.

Another factor must be introduced into the proposed formula, resulting from the hermeneutic process. In light of Bakhtin's literary theory, it seems that *musar* comedy must also have a "carnivalesque" component, which refers to the crossing of lines and challenging of conventional social norms. The carnivalesque challenges the social order and gives freedom to depressed powers and disadvantaged groups in a society. It goes beyond what is expected and what is right and accepts confusing or puzzling situations. This study finds that *musar* comedies do include carnivalesque components, even though, on the surface, they seem to be dealing with protagonists who obey the social conventions. How is that possible? How can a tale both confirm and subvert collective values at one and the same time? The paradox aptly explains the purpose and interaction of these unconventional, often bawdy, grotesque, or even repugnant *musar* tales amid the nonnarrative, normative, ethical prose. The carnivalesque was a powerful element that drew readers into the inner world of the text, affected them emotionally, influenced them, and caused them to amend their behaviors. It is the internal powerhouse of *musar* literature, although it is latent and may only be found and analyzed through a process of interpretation.

How is the carnivalesque component concealed in these didactic texts? It hides within the musar tales and, especially, in the dialogue between the folktales and their ethical, contextual prose frameworks. The latent carnivalesque potential of the embedded comedies was essentially evoked when the *musar* tales merged with the *musar* prose. The premodern readers were not actually aware of this internal dialogue, between the overt and the covert, which is now being revealed by postmodern reading and interpretation. For this reason, postmodern readings are important tools for describing, explaining, and understanding the powerful influence those texts had on their reading audience.

For instance, the pious man who was transformed into a wet nurse to breastfeed his baby crossed gender boundaries. The typical, conservative thinking, characteristic of premodern readership, only recognized two clearly defined genders that were wholly distinct. This tale touched the readers' darkest fears by breaking the rules of nature in a very intimate way. Such a transformation, the main character changed into some type of androgynous creature, an aberrant monster, featuring both male and female organs, likely made readers anxious.

The obedient son, who abided by his father's will, went on a long journey, leaving his pregnant wife at home for many years. The first part of the story suggests that he ran away from all his marital and familial responsibilities, abandoning his wife and his unborn child, to become an irresponsible adventurer, a life about which many male readers might fantasize. Then, in the last part of the plot, the returning husband erroneously suspects that his wife is cheating on him with a younger man—who, it turns out, is his adult son, whom he had never met. Thus the tale raises the issue of infidelity in marriage, an unforgivable sin and a social aberration, even if a plausible theme in literary fiction. This suspected act of adultery is particularly egregious, since it involves a younger man, entailing innuendos of lust and sex. Of course, it all turns out to be a false alarm, but even the suspicion of adultery was a bold element in the plot.

The tale of the pious, poor man granted six years of good fortune also has a carnivalesque dimension, atypically reversing the traditional gender hierarchy, with the wife rather than the husband presented as the powerful spouse, the decision maker, in the marriage and the family. She gives her husband permission to engage in a dialogue with Elijah, and she is the one who tells their younger son to report all the charitable expenses. She is also the one who saves her husband and her family when Elijah returns six years later.

The story about the wife of the High Priest, who could not get pregnant, is another fantastic tale. Though it deals specifically with the purification ritual required for Jewish women before intercourse, it is primarily about the wife herself: her efforts to complete the ritual perfectly; her encounter with the angel Metatron; and her successful delivery of a baby who, strangely enough, resembles the Metatron rather than the father.

While all this may be explained in terms of the Jewish ethos, nonetheless, a carnivalesque reading of this tale evokes the fantastic imagery of a divine birth and gives the next-generation protagonist, R. Ishmael, a semiangelic identity.

The tale of the two merchants is written like a practical joke—initially, the injured merchant is presented as a loser who forfeits his ocean voyage due to a minor injury, whereas in the latter part of the tale he becomes a winner. His bad luck turns out to be good luck when reality is overturned and certain death is averted. The carnivalesque component here is found in the unexpected, fast shifts, with no promise of divine reward or suggestion of ethical logic. It raises questions like: What did the injured merchant do that caused him to be saved? What was the sin of his friend, for which the penalty was drowning at sea? Why would the author choose to have the fellow merchant die? The text does not provide any answers and the reader has no clue. Thus the story shows the arbitrary side of life, where one does not search for hidden realities, but just looks at what is there—random coincidences.

Finally, the tale of the miserable, solitary man who read only one rabbinic volume throughout his entire, long life, deals with lust and sexuality, when the dying man believes he is with a beautiful woman on his deathbed and follows her into Heaven. Is this his personal fantasy? Is he hallucinating? Is he losing his mind? Or is God rewarding him for his acceptance of his lot in life and steady faithfulness by means of some "kabbalistic embodiment," as described by Elliot R. Wolfson.[37] The reader cannot know for sure, but may learn to equate serious Torah studies with the fulfillment even of earthly desires in the afterlife (thus encouraging Jewish scholarship and adherence to the Torah). Or perhaps a scandalous or alien carnivalesque suggestion is manifested in this case, in which the prize for ongoing Torah studies is an encounter with—who knows what she is?—a beautiful female foreigner, a gentile stranger, a seductress, or a female demon, and is comparable to going to Heaven.[38] There are other cautionary Jewish tales (*musar* tragedies) that incorporate the notion that foreign women, female strangers, are always pretty and seductive and are sometimes she-demons. Any encounter with a strange woman raises the specter of transgression.

ספר
שבט מוסר

Figure 8. Sheveṭ Musar, Sudylkiv 1821, title page. Courtesy of the Rare Book Collection at Bar-Ilan University.

Out of context, many of these subtexts appear bold, crass, and unorthodox; one might think them unpalatable to the premodern reader. Within the framework of the *musar*, however, these provocative transgressions can be understood to provide something wanted and needed. Modern, critical reading and interpretation, following Bakhtin's directives, discloses the authors' sexual impulses, complexes, and fantasies, as well as those of their readers.

The next chapter focuses on exemplary Hebrew social tales using the same approach. The selected *musar* tales are presented along with the guiding formula and their new readings.

4

MUSAR SOCIAL EXEMPLA

Social issues are the butter and bread of ethical agendas. This chapter focuses on a group of tales that fall in the category of social exempla, straddling the fine line between the secular and the sacred.[1] Compared with the *musar* tales discussed thus far, these tales are extreme, both in their tendency to move on and off that line and owing to their inclination toward secularity, since they relate to social issues without any reference to anything transcendent. Strangely enough, although they are secular, universal, and neutral in regard to theology, they are nonetheless embedded in popular Jewish religious essays,[2] where folklore and ethical instruction merge in a dialogue. Three questions guide the current chapter: What influence does this interaction between folklore and pedantic ethical prose have on *musar* literature in general? How do the embedded folktales impact each *musar* work as a whole? What is the effect of this amalgamation on the readership?

Regarding the embedded folktales, we know that most of them, if not all, were adapted from other languages (Arabic, Greek, Latin, and various European vernaculars), and they are largely secular in nature, presumably void of religious content, featuring allegedly universal plots. What, then, makes them folktales? The folkloric classification is determined first by the ways in which they were disseminated and, later on, by the nature and means of their documentation in each specific culture (oral reiterations, handwritten manuscripts, or published works). To determine this, scholars seek evidence of "multiple existence," as defined by Eli Yassif following Alan Dundes.[3] The presence of similar artistic renditions or variations of the same artistic tale in more than one work is an indication of its popularity, wide recognition, and acceptance by the readers, indicating that it has acquired the status of public property or even become a cliché—a fixed metaphor.

Among Orthodox Jewry to this day, *musar* texts play an important role in everyday life, especially for the men, but most women and children are familiar with them as well. This *musar* literature is meant to serve as leisure reading, consistent with the Jewish ethos and the Jewish way of life, though it is also included among *sifrē qodesh* (sacred books). These books generally deal with virtues and their primary purpose was and is to foster the Jewish way of life through ethical instruction.

The category of social exempla was adapted for use in this study from the well-known medieval genre. An exemplum (or an exemplary tale) is a short story written to teach a lesson in morality. It is always accompanied by an ethical text or is embedded within a *musar* anthology. Although *musar* exempla are primarily designed to demonstrate an idea concerning virtue and to persuade readers to mend their ways, they were also supposed to be entertaining (so they might be memorable) and to serve as paradigms for dealing with life's problems.[4] Amid the large group of didactic tales embedded in the *musar* literature—all of which may be referred to as *musar* exempla—it is possible to distinguish a smaller subgroup, focused on social hierarchies, denoted "social exempla." The tales in that subgroup relate specifically to anonymous protagonists and present short anecdotes from everyday life, especially secular stories about social dilemmas.[5]

The themes of *musar* social exempla are usually culturally neutral and universal, transcending time and space, and presented as human situations in nonspecific Jewish contexts. This chapter will demonstrate how those folktales become charged with the Jewish cultural ethos when embedded in the broader Jewish context: each *musar* work is firmly anchored by real details about the author, the specific Jewish community, and so on. Moreover, there are usually a few paratexts (surrounding printed matter) that also charge the *musar* text with sacred connotations:

The spirit of the title.
The contents of the book's title page.
The contents of the prologue or epilogue, where one may find the author's declaration about the message or intent of the book, its goals, its sources, and, perhaps, a profile of the targeted readership.

A few textual features may also transform the text into a sacred work:

Rhetoric: the use of biblical verses and rabbinic citations as proofs in support of the arguments.
Contents: the use of didactic contents rephrased in terms of dos and don'ts.
Messages: theological messages, especially those related to divine reward and punishment.

These findings align with Hans Robert Jauss's theory on the acceptance of the literary text via the history of reception. Jauss was interested in the relationship between literature and history and, more precisely, the interaction between production and reception in a historical context. According to Jauss, history and aesthetics are integrated.[6] Thus, it may be argued that sacred texts are characterized by features that are almost universal and have been replicated by many authors in many geographic regions over hundreds of years. It is that very repetition that makes the *musar* social exempla so easy to recognize as the unique subgroup that stood at the forefront of the Jewish literary heritage during the premodern period and became accepted by Jewish readers in the centuries that followed.

Furthermore, the Jewish rituals, customs, and habits implied by the act of reading per se also rendered *musar* literature sacred. As previously noted, Pierre Bourdieu coined the term "habitus," which refers to human behavior that becomes habitual. According to Bourdieu, the habitus is created through daily practice; it is manifested in regular human actions, and always serves a practical function in a historical context; that is, human actions are grounded in a certain culture against a specific historical background. He explains that habitus is a system of durable, transposable dispositions, structured to generate and organize practices and representations that may be adapted without conscious design—since habits tend to become a way of life. Those dispositions are not a result of obedience to official or statutory rules or products of an organized action; on the contrary, they are inherited unintentionally and are dominant in certain groups, social classes, and subcultures, as a result of the desires to conform and belong.[7]

To identify those rituals that are a part of the Jewish habitus of perusing, purchasing, and reading premodern *musar* literature, one should ask the following questions: (1) Who owns the book? (2) Who knows how to read the book? (3) Why do people read the book? (4) When do people read the book? (5) How do community leaders treat the book? (6) How was the book treated throughout the generations of its readers?

The answers to these questions imbue each *musar* text—as well as the folktales embedded within—with additional meanings, with a specific Jewish cultural attitude, such that the folktale contributes to the overall perspective. Thus from a narratological point of view, one may identify a group of voices that are external to the text. The first voice, which is a collective one, is that of the ancient sources that sustained the folktale and documented it, some of them not necessarily Jewish. The second is that of the narrator of the folktale, using a metaphor to say something about human behavior. The third is that of the narrator of the didactic, nonfictional *musar* text, who provides the prologue and epilogue that imbue the story with its Jewish atmosphere. The fourth and final voice is that of the biblical and rabbinic references located in the prologue and epilogue.

These voices compete in regard to the meaning of the folktale and the quality of the readers' attention, encouraging readers simply to enjoy an enjoyable folktale or to ponder ethical questions. It is the authors' didactic arguments that formulate and frame the Jewish spirit of the folkloric plots and make them appropriate for the Jewish reader, allowing the easy incorporation of carnivalesque themes into Jewish culture.

To reiterate, the special genre of *musar* social exempla straddles the boundary between the sacred and the secular when it presents an exemplary tale flexible enough to accommodate a theological interpretation.

Table 3. Social Exempla Found in Premodern *Musar* Literature

Rhetorical technique	Radicalization
Rhetorical mode	Allegory
Tone	Neutral, sometimes humorous
Contents	Social classes, social hierarchies, and social administration
Reach of the literal plot	Secular, universal
Existence of God or divine justice	None indicated
Contextual frame and paratexts	Inferred religious Jewish contexts and associations, emphasizing the special conduct of the Jewish people (the "chosen people") and the expectation of divine punishments and rewards

This flexibility is not a feature of the literal plot but exists in the abstract ability to merge its narrative into many kinds of textual contexts, including sacred ones. Table 3 lists the common denominators of this genre of folktales when transplanted into *musar* texts.

As in the previous chapters, this chapter introduces a modest selection of tales, and the literary and folkloristic analyses and modern readings follow.

Choosing a Suitable Groom

This social exemplum is in the chapter on flattery in the sixteenth-century *musar* work, *Orḥot Ṣaddiqim*.

> Once there was a wealthy and pious merchant, who had one daughter. When it was time for her to wed, the father sought the best man he could find to marry her. At the end of his search, he could not decide between the two final candidates, and he asked his best friend to help him choose. The father and the friend pretended that they were quarreling over something and asked the two young men who was right. The first immediately supported the father

and even lied to help him win the debate. The second, in contrast, would not lie and told the truth. The father chose for his daughter the one who would not lie.

This tale, a typical social exemplum, promotes the virtue of integrity and condemns flattery, by serving as an entertaining literary tool for the self-explanatory presentation and illustration of the subject under discussion, bolstered by the ideas presented in the context of that chapter's ethical prose. The prologue refers to the prohibition against flattering people, even family members. The epilogue uses this social exemplum to further another, more specific, issue: the flattery of community leaders, which is a related matter, since the plot talks about a situation in which a person from a lower social status—one potential groom—flatters someone from a higher social status—the bride's father, a wealthy merchant. The candidate's lower status is suggested by his efforts to flatter this man of standing in the community, who may become his future father-in-law.

In the hierarchical structure of Jewish society at that time, the bride's father was the one who would support the young couple financially, so this relationship is at issue. However, in the context of European folktales, this story is presented as a test of fidelity, appearing in many renditions, classified in the *Motif Index of Folk Literature* (ST) as motif H338 "Faithfulness as Suitor Test" and also listed in the ATU.[8] This plot is subsumed by the familiar metastructure of a larger group of folktales dealing with wisdom and court trials: in cases in which a judge is uncertain of the correct verdict, he uses a psychological strategy to uncover the liar or the imposter.[9]

We can guess why this theme is so popular in folktales. First of all, it raises the question of the basic trust between people and the ethics of crossing lines to help a loved one. Second, it suggests the irrevocability of marriage in traditional societies—a binding decision.[10] The tale is blatantly out of context since it describes a secular situation within a sacred text. Not only is God absent, but there is no hint of any divine justice, nor providence. These characters are left to solve their own problems. This thought leads to the next example, another well-known folktale.

The King and the Candle

As previously mentioned in chapter 1, this folktale first appeared in the eleventh-century work entitled *Tiqun Middot ha-Nefesh*, by Ibn Gabirol, originally written in Arabic and translated into Hebrew by Ibn Tibbon a hundred years later.

> ONCE THERE WAS A KING who hosted many guests, and when night came, they all went to sleep. After several hours, the king woke up and in the middle of the night, he trimmed the candle wick, so that it would not burn out. His servants came to him, saying: "Why didn't you order us to take care of the candles?" And the King answered his servants: "I woke up as a king and I'm still a king."

In accordance with folklore's "multiple existence" principle, this folktale has many versions in Jewish *musar* literature. For example, there are renditions in *Iggeret ha-Musar* [The letter on morality] by Shem-Ṭov b. Joseph ibn Falaquera (ca. 1225–95, Spain); *Magen Avot* [The shield of the Patriarchs] by R. Shim'on b. Ṣemaḥ Duran (1361–1444, Spain); and *Ṣemaḥ ṣaddiq* by R. Leon of Modena (1571–1648, Italy), among others. There is also another version in *Orḥot Ṣaddiqim*. The virtue promoted in this tale is modesty. The king, as a literary figure, serves as a trope, that is, a rhetorical device for explaining modesty in a tangible way. When read without any preconceptions, its plot is totally secular. It contains nothing that alludes to any sacred message; the sacred is introduced only by means of the prologue and the epilogue. In other words, the transcendent potentiality for the folkloric plot is conveyed via the nonfictional contents of the *musar* text.

Furthermore, reading both the context and the embedded, framed tale narrows the hermeneutic potential of the metaphor, affixing it to the very specific contextual frame of divine reward and punishment in the afterlife. The following is some of the biblical context found in *Tiqun Middot ha-Nefesh*, chapter 2, part 1 of the prologue:

> The Prophets said: "I am nothing but dust and ashes" (Gen. 18:27), and they said: "I am nothing but a worm and not a man" (Ps. 22:7).

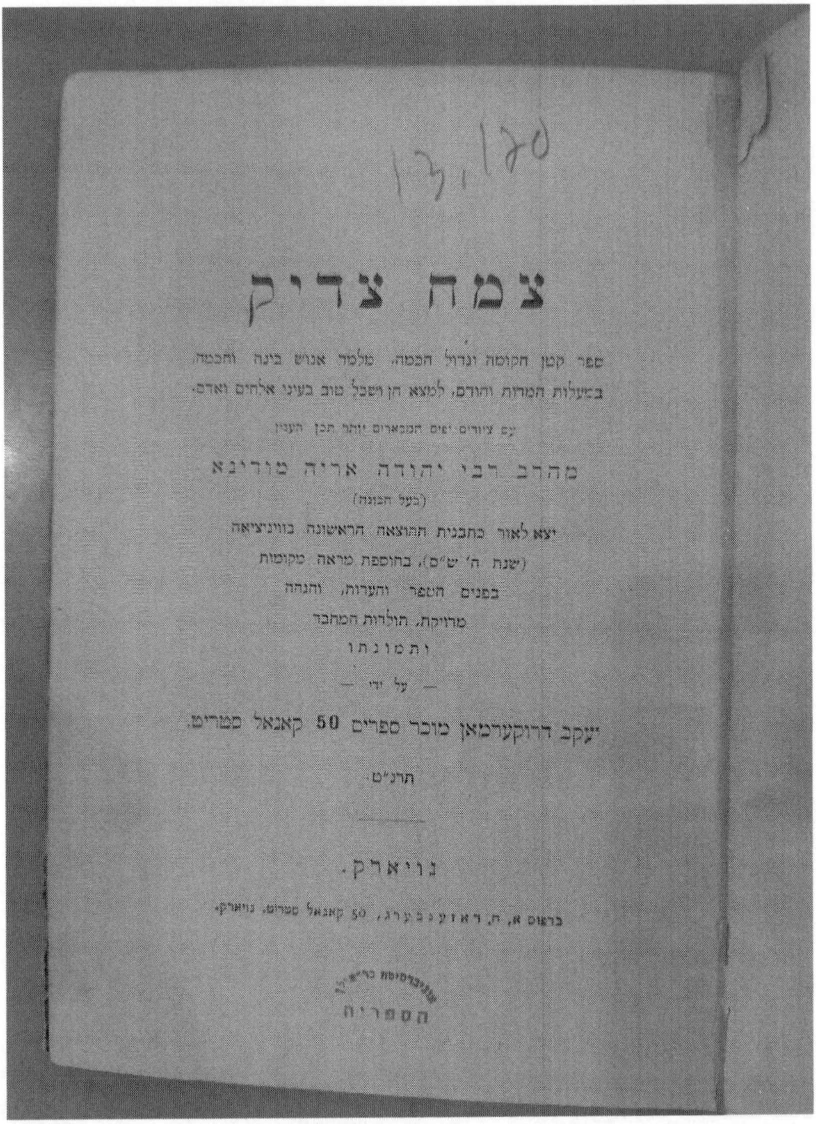
צמח צדיק

ספר קטן הקומה וגדול הכמה, מלמד אנוש בינה וחכמה
במעלות המדות והודם, למצא חן ושכל טוב בעיני אלהים ואדם.

עם ציורים יפים המבארים יותר תכן הענין

מהרב רבי יהודה אריה מודינא
(בעל הבונה)

יצא לאור כתבנית ההוצאה הראשונה בווינציאה
(שנת ה' ש"ם), בהוספת מראה מקומות
בפנים הספר והערות, והגהה
מדויקת, תולדות המחבר
ותמונתו
— על ידי —
יעקב דרוקערמאן מוכר ספרים 50 קאנאל סטריט.

תרנ"ט.

נויארק.

בדפוס א. ה. ראזענבערג, 50 קאנאל סטריט, נויארק.

Figure 9. Ṣemach Ṣaddiq, New York 1899, title page. Courtesy of the Rare Book Collection at Bar-Ilan University.

> And the Prophets gained praise for their behavior. And thus, people should know that modesty is rewarded. . . . Therefore, the modest person earns a just reward and that reward is respect and wealth.

Note that this specific prologue is based on biblical verses, whereas in other cases, a prologue may be built on rabbinic references to reward. The reward mentioned in the biblical verses is, of course, divine, thus this rhetoric automatically brings God into the frame. Though God is not present in the plot, the idea of the all-seeing God, who judges humanity (as written in Psalms [33:13]: "The Lord looks down from Heaven. He sees all Mankind" and Proverbs [12:14]: "One is repaid in kind for one's deeds") is insinuated into the tale by means of the prologue. Thus the whole text is framed in a theological context, although the folktales themselves are neutral.

The King Who Was Afraid to Get Angry

The third *musar* social exemplum discussed here focuses on a king's awareness of his weaknesses and his determination to moderate his own behavior, showing a degree of maturity and the internalization of the need to contain his excessive anger. It appears in the chapter that deals with pride in *Tiqun Middot ha-Nefesh*, by Ibn Gabirol.

> AND IT WAS TOLD THAT a king gave one of his slaves a letter and ordered him: "When you see me angry, hand me this letter immediately." And in the letter, it was written: "You should withdraw yourself from your anger, because you are not divine; you are human, flesh and blood, and soon you are going to die and become dust and food for worms and maggots."

Though this tale praises a single king, between the lines one can sense criticism of the way many rulers apparently act toward their subjects, which is probably the reason that this king commands a slave, rather than someone in the royal family or a courtier. The plot also emphasizes the existence of a social hierarchy, the enormous difference in status between the two figures, so it meets the criteria of an exemplum. The same plot, with minor changes, is also found in other *musar* works; for instance, in *Orḥot Ṣaddiqim*, this social exemplum, with an added episode, is found in the chapter on forgetfulness.

> THERE ONCE WAS A KING WHO gave one of his slaves a letter and ordered him to save that letter and to hand it back to him whenever the slave saw him getting angry. And in the letter, it was written: "You should know that you are not God, but only an expendable body that will be eaten by worms from end to end, until only worms and maggots remain." And the king commanded the same slave to stand before him whenever he ordered that a person be lashed with whips of fire and to declaim those words, so his angry heart might be subdued.

It is interesting to note that this tale is in the chapter on "obliviousness," which emphasizes the tendency to forget one's place in the world or to forget that everyone eventually dies. The additional episode depicting the slave standing before his master, the king, and reading the letter to him, while the king is torturing another human being, enhances the drama of the plot. Moreover, it provides a concrete example of very objectionable behavior by rulers toward their subjects, which the exemplum implies should be condemned. Another version of this same tale is located in *Mivḥar ha-Peninim*, also ascribed to Ibn Gabirol; it is the shortest rendition, but quite clear and direct.

> THERE WAS A KING WHO HAD a young slave. And the king ordered the slave to stand in front of him whenever he beat his subjects with whips and to tell him: "Your majesty, remember the Last Judgment."

Note that this version mentions the theological concept of the Last Judgment at the end of days, a belief that relates to reward and punishment after death and the resurrection of the souls when the Messiah comes. These eschatological notions move the plot from a humanistic to a theological reading, a reading that implies a world order whose ultimate value is justice.

The Greedy and the Envious

The next *musar* tale condemns hatred so intense that a person is even willing to commit self-harm just to ensure that his or her nemesis is also wretched. This tale, which also falls under the category of social exempla, employs a grotesque plot, just to make its point. This absurd case is so illogical that it verges on becoming a humorous anecdote. It is found in the chapter that deals with envy in *Orḥot Ṣaddiqim*.

> A GREEDY MAN AND AN ENVIOUS MAN met a king, who told them: "I give you permission to ask me anything. One of you will ask for something and will get it, while the other will get twice as much of the same thing." The envious man decided not to ask for anything, because he knew that his friend would get twice as much, and that he would envy him. The greedy man did not know what to ask for, because he wanted to get double of anything the other would request. As such, the greedy man persuaded the envious man to ask first. In the end, the envious man decided to ask the king to stab him in one eye, so that the king would stab both the greedy man's eyes.

In the context of the chapter, this tale is read allegorically, since this king seems to have an abnormal desire to give people whatever they want without any compensation—like a Jewish Santa Claus, giving gifts and fulfilling wishes. Unfortunately, these two characters waste their chance to derive benefit by choosing to hurt one another, so they both get hurt. The miraculous motif of "reward—any wish will be granted" (*ST*, Q-115)—in this ethical exemplum turns into a fools' contest, ending in failure and loss for both sides. Both sides are condemned to suffer, in accordance with the message of the *musar* contextual framing, which warns against the vice of envy.

Death of a Scholar's Sons for a Lie

The following tale is an adaptation of this rabbinic tale found in the Babylonian Talmud, *Sanhedrin* 97a, in Aramaic.

> CONCERNING THE LACK OF TRUTH, Rava said: "Initially, I would have said that there is no truth anywhere in the world. However, there was a certain Sage, and some said his name was Rav Tavut though others called him Rav Tavyomē, who was so honest that, even if they were to offer him the entire world, his words would still not deviate from the truth. But he told me: 'One time, I happened to come to a certain place, and Truth was its name, and its residents would never deviate from the truth, and no person there would die prematurely. I married a local woman, and she bore me two sons. One day, while my wife was washing her hair, a neighbor knocked on the door. I thought it was improper conduct to tell the neighbor that my wife was bathing, so I told her my wife wasn't at home. Since I did not tell the truth, both my sons died. The people living in that place came to me asking what this meant. I told them the nature of the incident and what happened as a result. So they asked me to leave their place, so as not to bring premature death upon them'."[11]

This rabbinic legend was adopted by authors of Hebrew *musar* texts and is found in the chapter on innocence in *Ma'alot ha-Middot* and also in the chapter on lying in *Ṣemaḥ ṣaddiq*. In the former the protagonist is anonymous, and in the latter the protagonist is named Rav Tavut. The *Ma'alot ha-Middot* version introduces minor changes in the talmudic tale, especially by omitting the scholar's name and describing the woman as "combing her hair." A brief anecdote about the changes in the text concerns the place where the episode occurred. In the Talmud, where the version is in Aramaic, the place is called *Qushṭa*, which means "truth" in Aramaic. In the *Ma'alot ha-Middot* version, which is in Hebrew, the place is still named *Qushṭa*, which was actually the Hebrew name for Constantinople, which, from both Jewish and non-Jewish perspectives, was a very important cultural hub. These two versions also serve to demonstrate that the various renditions of the same literary theme found in different *musar* texts may be very much alike, displaying only minor deviations.

> ONCE THERE WAS A SCHOLAR who said: "No one always tells the truth." Another scholar said to him that, even if he was offered all the money in the world, he would not lie. Once, he had arrived in a place named Qushṭa, where people always tell the truth and, thus, had very long lives. He married a local woman, and she gave birth to two sons. One day, when she was washing and combing her hair, suddenly one of her female neighbors came by and knocked on the door. The scholarly husband thought that there was no way he might open the door, without the neighbor seeing his wife with her hair loose; so, he told her that his wife was not in. After this, both his sons died. Then, the residents of Qushṭa came and asked him: "What is this and how can this happen? What sin did you commit to cause both your sons to die?" So, the scholar told them all that had happened. Then, the angry locals ordered him to leave, saying: "Get out of here! We're afraid you may bring a plague upon us."

The tale deals with a social problem or, more accurately, a convention that exists among the members of a particular society—the extreme requirement for complete honesty at all times; after all, to the average reader, a man saying his wife was not at home seems like a little white lie, not involving any serious ethical issue. However, in Qushṭa, the protagonist is presented as someone who not only concedes, admitting his sinful mistake (which has tarnished Qushṭa's good reputation for total honesty), but who even accepts the extreme fate of the death of his sons as his due punishment. It is not divine punishment that makes this tale a social exemplum, but rather the severity of the social ramifications of his lie that is the overriding consideration.

There are many legends in Jewish tradition that relate the sudden death of two sons, and they all try to come to grips with the concept of divine justice. Of all the human experiences that relate to theodicy, the death of innocent children without any apparent reason is one of the most traumatic that adults share. The specific crises of parents coping with the untimely death of a child has always been a part of reality. It is no surprise that those kinds of tragedies have occupied the human mind from ancient times and have given rise to folktales relating to them. Every culture has legends and folktales that try to come to terms with such events: How do children die? Why does this happen? What should readers learn from this kind of event?

Resolving this issue is a major key to finding the meaning of life, as well as the meaning of death; otherwise, there might be no significance to good or bad human conduct. Aaron the Levite, brother of Moses, lost two sons on the same day (Lev. 10:1–2), but their deaths were direct punishments for their own regrettable actions. When Aaron learned that they had died because of the sin they had committed, he reacted with unusual restraint: "And Aaron was silent" (Lev. 10:3). A similar tale describes the sons of R. Meir, who were both buried under a wall that fell. According to some versions, they were saved, since their father did not desecrate the Shabbat by trying to rescue them from under the ruins. Since he kept the Shabbat, he was rewarded, and they did not die.[12]

However, in the context of a *musar* text, this plot becomes a social exemplum, because it omits the theological content and focuses on the human behavior not directed toward God but rather toward other people. This is a classic example of how a literary theme may go in several directions, depending on its framing by the *musar* text. The author takes advantage of the genre's flexibility, which allows him to extend the boundaries of the tale to better accommodate the Jewish message of the ethical, nonfictional prose.

Like the other tales discussed in this chapter, all exhibiting the characteristics identified in table 3, "Death of the Scholar's Sons for a Lie" can be classified as a social exemplum. As the table exhibits, exaggeration was a popular rhetorical technique in *musar* works, manifested in this tale by the sudden death of the married scholar's two sons, owing to what was a seemingly harmless white lie told to a neighbor. The extreme price paid by the father as divine punishment for his social treason was, indeed, quite an exaggerated consequence. Nonetheless, as noted, *musar* authors often intentionally seek to elicit the readers' fear in order to make their

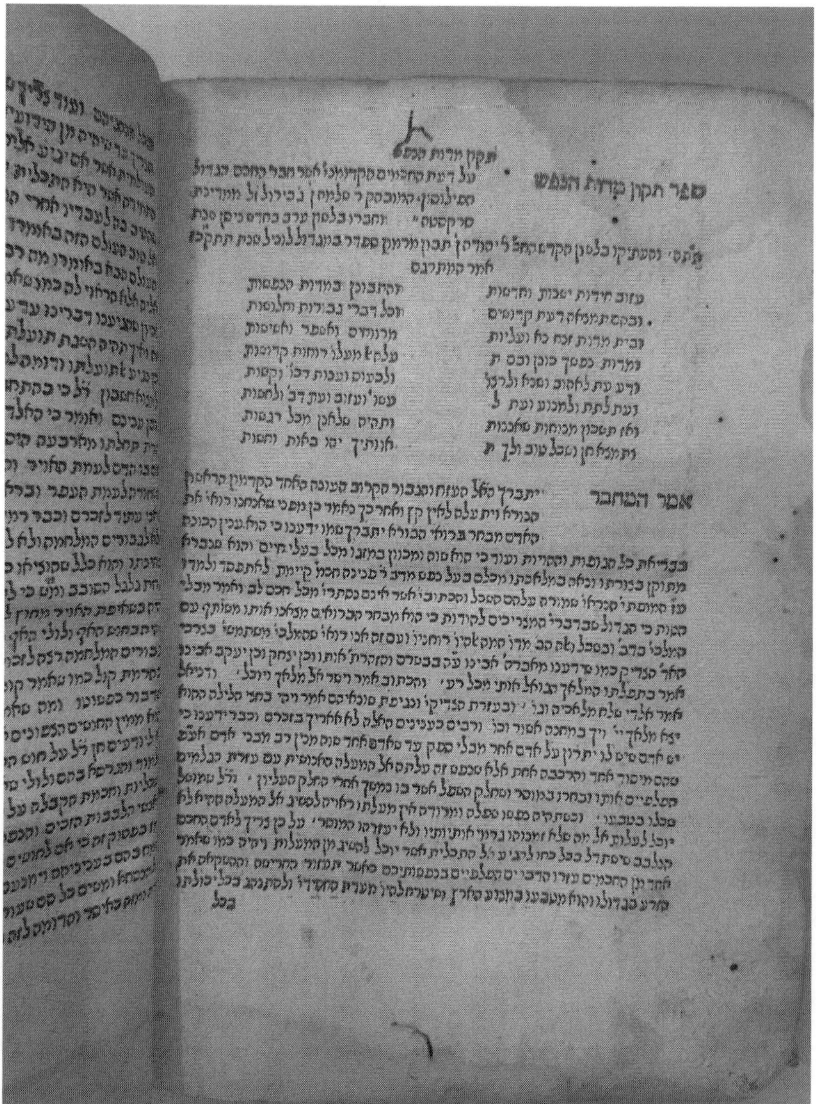
ספר תקון מדות הנפש

אמר המחבר

Figure 10. Tiqun Middot ha-Nefesh, Constantinople 1550, author's prologue. Courtesy of the Rare Book Collection at Bar-Ilan University.

didactic messages more unforgettable—a pedagogical tactic employed by this embedded social exemplum.

In addition, this tale in its context is a classic case of the significant interplay between tale and nonfictional prose, the tale's general telos combining with the surrounding text to animate each of the following elements: 1) the thrust of the tale itself, which promotes interpersonal honesty; 2) the *musar* chapter's subtheme discussing the sin of lying; 3) the entire *musar* chapter that discusses innocence; and 4) the entire *musar* work, dealing with vices and virtues. The interpenetration of these levels of meaning and purpose within the *musar* literature is what turns the *musar* tale into a genre of its own.

5

THE ALLEGORICAL *MUSAR* TALE

The allegory was the most frequently seen type of *musar* tale found in medieval and premodern *musar* literature. According to Meyer H. Abrams, an 'allegory' is "a narrative, whether in prose or in verse, in which the agents and actions, and sometimes the setting as well, are contrived by the author to make coherent sense on a 'literal' or primary level of signification and, at the same time, to signify a second, correlated order of signification."[1] Their representation among *musar* tales is not surprising, since allegories have been a major rhetorical tool in didactic literature ever since. *Musar* texts closely follow in the footsteps of ancient rabbinic literature, influenced also by non-Jewish conventions from the ancient, medieval, and premodern periods.

Fear of punishment and expectations of reward, in both this world and in the afterlife, taught through the generations, led to the creation of a very large collection of tales that, together, provided a theological frame for the belief in divine reward and punishment for one's actions and even one's thoughts. Often, in fiction as well as in real life, what one sees is not necessarily what one gets, since the impossibility of cosmological knowledge limits human ability to analyze any specific temporal situation. Ordinary human beings cannot comprehend eternal judgment so, sometimes, "rewards" and "punishments" are not what they seem.

This chapter discusses narrative traditions whose metasubject is theodicy—that is to say, traditional narratives that deal with the problem of evil and suffering in the world. Theodicy attempts to resolve the seeming contradiction between the simultaneous presence of an omnipotent God and the existence of evil in the mundane world. In other words, theodicy grapples with the concept of divine justice. Resolving this issue is a key to finding meaning in life; without an understanding of divine justice, there might be no significant justification or motivation for ethical conduct. It would not be an exaggeration to say that theodicy is fundamental to the development and acceptance of social norms and the maintenance of social order.

The term "theodicy" was first coined in 1710 by German philosopher Gottfried Wilhelm von Leibniz (1646–1716). Since then, philosophers and sociologists, including Max Weber (1864–1920), John Hick (1922–2012), and Peter L. Berger (1929–2017) have discussed this concept in light of the early works of the Greek bishop St. Irenaeus (130–202) and the theologian, St. Augustine of Hippo (354–430). All in all, theodicy has been one of the most formidable challenges facing theologians and philosophers since the days of antiquity.

Isaiah (55:9) illustrates the gap between the human and the divine: "For as the heavens are higher than the earth, so are my ways higher than your ways, and my thoughts higher than your thoughts." This notion is reflected in several biblical tales, most particularly in the Book of Job. Other examples of perplexing issues of reward and punishment may be seen in the stories of Cain murdering Abel (Gen. 4:1–15), the death of Jephthah's daughter (Judg. 11:31, 34, 39), and the death of Uriah (2 Sam. 11:17).

One of the main philosophical obstacles to a satisfying explanation of divine justice is the limits of human understanding. It may be virtually impossible to describe God's laws in human terms. Humans can perceive reality only with their five corporeal senses on the physical planet Earth during their limited lifetimes, when they are able to observe evil, sorrow, and injustice. How, then, may they be convinced that divine justice might be meted out across a much greater sphere over unlimited time? Folk traditions addressed this conundrum—how to describe the divine in human terms—by the massive development of narrative traditions that offer some kind of explanation, thus serving as sources of comfort and relief.[2] For common people, who have neither access to rare books nor the education needed to understand the philosophical discussions in them, such allegorical tales served both as a means of explanation and a source of solace.

The theodical legends included here are shaped as allegories, constructed around a fixed group of protagonists, usually a king and his servants, who represent God and his believers. Abrams distinguished between two main types of allegories: the "historico-political allegory" and the "allegory of ideas." Only the latter is found in *musar* texts. In this type, the protagonists and the plot represent an abstract doctrine or thesis that the allegory demonstrates by the personification of the vices and the virtues, the presentation of archetypal characters, and the promotion of certain attitudes.

The Pious Man and the Soldiers

This allegorical tale has many versions in *musar* literature. The version presented here appears in *Orḥot Ṣaddiqim* in the chapter that deals with the uniqueness of God.

> **Once a pious Jewish man was** walking on the road and saw many soldiers coming back from a war with their captive enemies and the rich spoils of war. And the pious man told them: "You are coming from a trivial war, but you should prepare yourself for the great war." So, they asked him: "What do you mean?" And the pious man answered: "The great war is the one to control your own impulses."

This tale could reflect a realistic situation occurring sometime during the premodern period, in which a Jew witnessed soldiers heading off to war and returning with captives and booty. In those days, the world of warfare was very far from Jewish life, and Jews, as a minority society, did not usually participate, though it was a major aspect of premodern civilization. Part of the reason for Jewish exclusion was that most of those wars were Christian or Islamic holy wars, in which Jewish men were forbidden to participate. However, in the above allegory, the pious Jew finds compensation for not being able to take part in this habitus by insinuating that he, too, is a warrior of sorts.[3] Although not a warrior fighting against other people, which he perceives to be something small and easy, he is rather a warrior battling against his innermost urges and impulses, which is much harder. This suggests that the pious Jewish man is, essentially, always waging war with himself. This military *musar* allegory depicts wars as being easy in comparison with the inner conflicts that pious, Jewish men must undergo and overcome. It also reflects the mindset that the *musar* author is trying to confer upon his readers—perhaps as a means of comforting them for not serving as "real," conventional soldiers.

The point here is that this tale may be read as an allegory on the essence of Jewish life and thought. In fact, the paragraphs that precede the allegory concludes a long passage of consolation, in which the author writes that, although a Jewish man cannot be a warrior in a real army, he is a warrior in the "Army of God." The iconic symbol in this tale is war, which becomes a metaphor for an individual's inner struggle to control his or her own, impulses, emotions, and deeds, as based on the well-known saying from the Mishnah, *Pirqē Avot* (4:1c): "Who is mighty? He who subdues his [or her] evil inclinations."

The Arrogant Prince

The following *musar* allegory, "The Arrogant Prince," which appears in different versions in other *musar* works, is in the chapter on piety in *Orḥot Ṣaddiqim*.

> **And this incident is similar** to the tale of a prince, who was one or two years old when he was kidnapped and taken very far away from his kingdom, perhaps a thousand parasangs[4] away. He was raised in a country house and was taught to live like a farmer. However, the prince did not remember that he was of royal blood, and he knew nothing about royalty. After he grew up, a member of his family came to him and told him that he was royal, but not to which royal family he belonged. On learning of this, the prince

> became a bit arrogant. Then, another man came to him and revealed the name of his father, telling him where to find his country and his kingdom. Then, this prince became even more arrogant, and wished to return to his kingdom; but he was afraid that, if he went, no one would recognize him and no one would remember him. But his father, the king, heard that his son was alive and sent messengers to him, and they recognized the prince by the way he looked. Then, the king sent ministers and royal attire to him. At that point, the prince became very arrogant. After he was dressed and mounted on the king's horse, his heart became a king's heart, and he became exceedingly arrogant.

This *musar* allegory is quite odd in the context of folktale narrative tradition. Readers were used to plots that had a defined ending, with rewards granted to the good protagonists and punishments meted out to the villains, and expected to recognize the good guys and the bad guys from the outset. However, in this case, what the prince represents remains unclear until halfway through the story, which is both unexpected and somewhat confusing for the readers.

It raises a couple questions, such as: What does being "arrogant" mean? Must a king have a sense of sovereignty? This plot is an amalgam of many folktale motifs and the classic adventure story that breeds cultural heroes like Moses and Odysseus.[5] The cultural narrative about a royal heir who lives as a child far away from luxury and wealth, and develops a modest and truthful personality, is well known. But here the prince is torn between his sense of high self-esteem and feelings of inferiority, because he is afraid that he will not be recognized and honored in his own kingdom. He assumes his princely role so quickly, perhaps thanks to his inherent royal genes.

Nonetheless, as this tale illustrates, the vices and virtues about which the *musar*'s nonfiction prose preaches are not always unambiguous when it comes to the tales themselves. "The Arrogant Prince" creates a provocative main character, although the *musar* author ignores the prince's controversial features and focuses on certain other points of interest, which serve as the core of the ethical message. Such allegorical tales were designed to convey a theological message. To understand that message, one must read these *musar* allegories in their contexts; it is these that—which generate this distinct genre. As with all the previous genres of *musar* tales described in this book, the nonfictional context plays a crucial role in the function of the allegory, and the allegory must be read as part of the whole textual picture.

Thus the prologue to this one presents a discussion on the soul and how one should devote oneself to rising to a higher spiritual plain. Encountering the tale in isolation, it is easy to think that the prince's conduct is bad, that he's a villain. However, once the epilogue determines that the prince symbolizes the soul, then in accordance with the prologue, the import of the tale seems to be that the soul should be encouraged to rise to a higher level. Since this soul (the prince) was unaware of its powers, it had to be guided to the upper realms. As such, the combined reading of the *musar* paratexts with the allegorical tale turns the first impression upside down, by suggesting that the prince (the guided soul) is, indeed, behaving as he should, and properly accepts elevation to a higher realm.

The Sailor's Wife

This allegorical tale is found in the second chapter of R. Jonah Gerondi's *Sha'arē Teshuvah*, which deals with the ways to restore someone's faith in God. The source of this tale is the rabbinic commentary on Ecclesiastes, *Midrash qohelet rabbah* 9:6.[6]

> The wife of a sailor was making herself pretty, so she painted her eyes, while her husband was away on the high seas. Her neighbors asked her: "Why are you making yourself pretty? Isn't your husband far away?" She answered them: "My husband is a sailor and, if the wind changes direction, he might return home right away, so I prefer to be ready for him at all times."

From the adjacent epilogue, we know that this tale is an allegory about a person on the day of his or her death; in essence, a Jew should be preparing throughout life for the day of death, the day of divine judgment.

According to the epilogue, people should live with the fear of God's justice throughout life, while awaiting inevitable death. Note that, in the allegory, the implied erotic relationship between the preening wife and her sailor husband seems to be transformed into a metaphor for the loving bond between the Jewish people and God, which is neither new nor uncommon in sacred Jewish sources and Jewish theology. However, the epilogue unexpectedly reverses the apparent literal situation, stating that the sailor-husband (symbolizing the God-fearing Jew) should always live in the fear of God, whereas his wife (symbolizing God) is not frightened at all—she is beautiful, feminine, and sensual, and will always be thrilled when her husband returns (welcoming all who repent). This unusual twist supports two aforementioned principles: that the embedded tales and their *musar* contexts are not always perfectly coordinated and that *musar* authors sometimes like to shock the reader into remembering the lesson.

In fact, this is an allegory that essentially portrays the death of observant Jews as a pleasurable experience, despite the serious and threatening tone of the epilogue. The midrashic source of the tale refers to the verse "Let my garments be always white, and let thy head lack no oil" (Eccles. 9:8), also alluding to the pure, unblemished white garb worn by the High Priests in the Holy of Holies in the Jerusalem Temple on Yom Kippur. Thus the sinless Jew is represented by white cloth in the midrash, embodied here by the sailor's wife herself. In *Sha'arē Teshuvah*, this allegory is more direct, and the text is no longer merely a homily on a single verse but rather has taken the format of a folktale extending across a wider context.

The King Who Bestowed Silk

The following *musar* tale, which is also a theological allegory, belongs to a large and familiar group of parables of the type known as *Mashal le-Melekh* (Parable for a king), which is very prominent in rabbinic literature and was also adopted by later authors of various kinds of didactic and *musar* literature. In these parables, the king usually represents God and the servants represent his believers.[7] This one is in Ibn Paquda's prologue to *Ḥovot ha-Levavot.*

Once there was a king who gave coils of silk to two of his servants and observed what they did with them. The enthusiastic and agile servant chose the best ones and then sorted out what remained, until he had three groups of coils. After sorting the coils, he made them into the best material that he could, and then went to expert artisans, who made him beautiful garments with special colors, which he wore before the king at various times. The foolish servant sold all the silk for as much as he could get and took the money to buy food and drink. When the king saw what the two servants had done with his gift, he promoted the wise one to be his advisor and he banished the fool to a faraway desert to live among his enemies.

From the epilogue to this allegory, the reader understands that the silk stands for the Torah, gifted to the people of Israel to test them. The wise and the erudite took the words of the Torah and sorted them into three categories: 1) sayings about spiritual learning and wisdom of the heart; 2) words about one's physical being and practical duties; and 3) historical information about all the past generations. Thus, a good Jew should be familiar with all three and should know how, where, and when to apply them. However, the foolish, uneducated Jew is confused and misuses the different words in Torah, not distinguishing their distinct values and instructions. Moreover, such a fool is likely to use Torah knowledge for mundane pleasures and thus will die unaware of having missed many opportunities, and will not have maximized the value and use of that divine gift.

This allegorical tale has the archetypal plot of the wise man and the fool, frequently found in folktales, in which a king initiates a competition or assigns a special task. Sometimes the winner gets to marry the king's daughter. Generally, the younger competitor, or the one who is thought to be the fool, reveals himself as being clever and wise.[8] However, in the present case, this folktale becomes an allegory for the relationship between God and his believers, and its romantic aura transforms into a lecture on Jewish life.

The Ungrateful Child and the Grateful Prisoner

The following allegorical tale is in the second chapter of *Ḥovot ha-Levavot.*

> A KIND MAN FOUND A BABY in the desert. He took the baby to his house and raised him as his own. He fed and clothed him and gave him all that he could, until the baby grew old enough to understand what the man had done for him. Then, this same kind man heard about a refugee who had been taken prisoner by an enemy, kept naked and starving, and the captors were asking a great deal of money for his release. The kind man convinced the captors to accept payment of a ransom to free their prisoner, and he brought the poor man to his home to take care of him; however, he gave the refugee a lot less than he had given the child. Yet the refugee was more grateful than the child, because the child had become accustomed to being treated well, so he did not comprehend the great generosity of this kind man.

Since the foundling baby was discovered in the desert, this allegory, which is rooted in the Pentateuch, relates to the people of Israel, who were often less than grateful to God and to Moses during their forty years wandering in the desert (Exod. 15:24; 16:2). It is an allegory of the relationship between God and his believers, who are so accustomed to the bounty He gives them that they often undervalue it. As such, it counsels the blessed believer to always behave like the freed refugee and not like the ungrateful child.

In Hebrew, the negative noun *assir* (prisoner) echoes the positive term *assir todah*, meaning "one who is grateful." This linguistic association enhances the allegorical message—the freed prisoner indeed shows more gratitude than the spoiled child. It also emphasizes the difference between the ways in which the foundling and the prisoner had been treated. Although the refugee received less than the foundling did, he was more grateful, indicating his pure and kind nature, whereas the unappreciative foundling was being immature, heartless, and inconsiderate.

The refugee was willing to stay under the kind man's roof, accepting his improved lot with love. It is well known that people sometimes spoil those they love, and this may be argued to be the case in the relationship between God and the Jewish people. However, God's indulgence doesn't excuse the Jews for exhibiting, when they do, childish ingratitude, or for losing sight of God's greatness.

In the wide world of folklore, many folktales and fantasy narratives provide opportunities for grateful characters to echo the good qualities of the charitable and selfless protagonists, and they are rewarded for offering their help and support, without any expectation of payment.[9] In certain other folktales, a contrast is drawn between the behavior of grateful characters and ungrateful ones.[10]

Just such a distinction between two groups of people concerning their loyalty and faith in the master can be seen in the New Testament parables of Jesus. Parables such as the one about the Good Samaritan (Luke 10:29–37) introduce the same character of the kind man as an example of caring and compassion toward strangers. An allegory is always an invitation to read a text on more than one level, bearing in mind that it embodies both an overt and a latent message. There is the explicit plot, clearly in front of the reader, which is usually a very simple one that focuses on a king or a ruler and his subjects. But underneath the surface, there is a theological idea, in our case a religious subtext concerning the relationship between humanity and God. It turns out to be more of a religious allegory than a social one.

The Drug of Life

Musar texts often raise stimulating historical as well as literary questions. In fact, one might use them as case studies or source materials to assess the dissemination of folktales, to determine the impact of printed books on culture, or to evaluate how the intermingling of genres may affect the way the Jewish readers relate to the *musar* texts as a whole.

The next tale, "The Drug of Life," is a theological allegory found in the chapter on defamation in *Orḥot Ṣaddiqim*, which is based on a legend from *Midrash vayiqra rabbah* 16:2.

Once, there was a man shouting in the street: "Who wants to buy the drug of life?" Many people gathered around him, and the man pulled out of his bag a copy of the Book of Psalms and showed the crowd the verse: "Who is the man who desires life, who loves days to see goodness? Guard your tongue from evil" [Ps. 34:13–14]. And when Rabbi Yannai saw this, he took the man and brought him to his house and gave him food and drink and charity. Then his students came and asked the rabbi: "Is this the first time you heard this verse? Why did you treat this man so well?" And Rabbi Yannai answered them: "I am familiar with the verse, but this man helped me pay attention to it for the first time. In the past, when I read the chapter, I did not feel the meaning of the words, but now I do. This man made the verses come alive, so from this day on I will be more careful with my words."

This story may well represent the essential function of folktales in *musar* literature. R. Yannai articulated the importance of isolating a single element and shedding a spotlight just on it, as well as paying special attention to the meaning of the words. This psychological and literary technique is what the Russian formalist school termed "defamiliarization," which means experiencing something familiar from a fresh, new perspective.[11] In fact, this is the same mechanism by which familiar tales may take on new perspectives, when presented in the context of a sermon or a *musar* text that draws special attention to the virtue or vice being illustrated by that allegorical tale.

Musar literature not only offers a way to acquire such virtues as honesty, kindness, love of God, or modesty by explanations and examples, it also warns one away from adopting vices, such as anger, pride, wickedness, and parsimony. In recent decades, Jewish *musar* literature has been at the center of interest of scholars from various disciplines. This particular cultural phenomenon is recognized to merit extra attention, because it is a fertile and still understudied field of investigation.[12]

The Jewish *musar* allegory stresses the relationship between God and his believers through literary themes that are not connected directly to theological issues by their overt plots. If the episodes they adopt are not

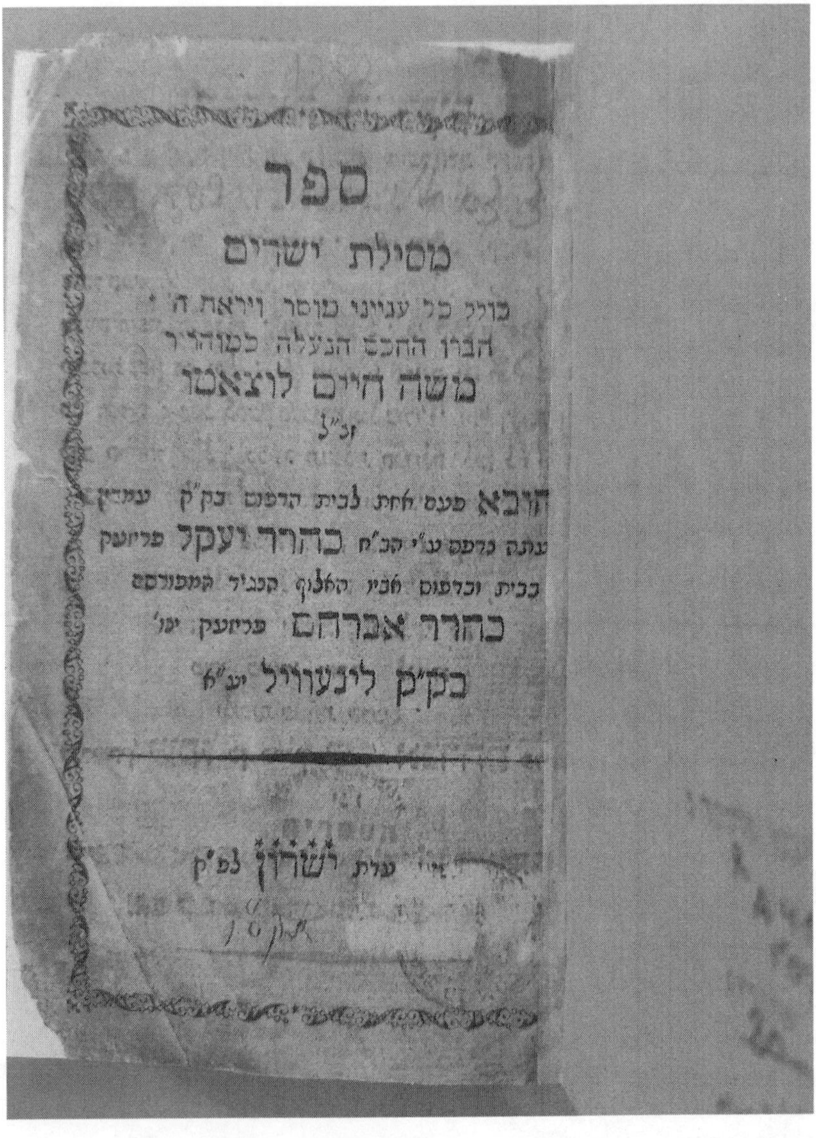

Figure 11. Mesillat Yesharim, Lunéville 1806, title page. Courtesy of the Rare Book Collection at Bar-Ilan University.

exactly frequent in mundane life, they nevertheless revolve around familiar human feelings, relationships, and conflicts, and it is these that are used to represent complex theological issues. Still, one should note that the believer, the reader of the text, is always being accused of thanklessness and indifference toward God and the existence of the afterlife. In contrast to *musar* tragedy or *musar* comedy, in which the reader is relatively passive, merely being counseled about the conduct of everyday life, the theological *musar* allegories attempt to create a sense of guilt in readers' minds. While *musar* tragedy is relatively melodramatic, sometimes threatening, and describes extreme situations, the *musar* allegory uses benign situations, common occurrences embodying common failings about which the reader must be forewarned.

CONCLUSIONS AND FINAL REMARKS

What is the significance of literary genres? And how do they affect musar readers? This book has sought to offer a conceptual frame for those folktales found embedded in premodern *musar* texts. The first goal was to place scholarly attention on this novel corpus as a whole. The second goal was to read and critique selected *musar* tales in a manner providing a conceptual frame for the categorization of the folkloric material in accordance with predetermined literary criteria. Finally, by means of a contextual, interactional metareading, it sought a deeper understanding of the specific literary and folkloric mechanisms at play in order to reach holistic interpretations of the tales from within their unique setting.

The mere choice of a certain literary genre is already a nonverbal, or preverbal, communication between the author and his or her reading audience; something is said by organizing the written message in a consistent and familiar way. Each genre has its own unique plot structure, repeats recognizable patterns, and makes use of literary conventions that assist the readers in making sense of unfamiliar plots. The *musar* authors did not invent the genres of tragedy, comedy, exemplum, and allegory, though they make good use of them. They chose appropriate folktales and reframed them to suit the *musar* mold, adjusting them to the Jewish way of thinking about vices and virtues. Then they embedded flexible, Judaized renditions of those representative tales into the didactic framework of the *musar* perspective.

The power of the folktale would not have been as great without the enormous impact of the printing press and the resulting wide distribution of books. Books serve all kinds of purposes. Some are meant to educate, to teach the reader how to cook, raise children, or achieve success. There are books that are meant to entertain, by eliciting amusement or, for some, engendering fear. Books document communities, journeys, and important people, or describe the world scientifically; others are meant to offer an aesthetic experience of human emotions. Some books are meant to explain other books (such as commentaries, dictionaries, and annotated editions).[1] The most important books in Western culture are, of course, the Hebrew Bible and the New Testament, which form the infrastructure for Western literature, art, folklore, liturgy, and more.

Books are instruments to document, reveal, and introduce the principal features of a given culture and, by doing so, some of them are designated as being canonic, indicating that not all books are equally prestigious in readers' eyes. Transactions in connection with books also mark sellers and collectors as individuals having certain cultural perspectives and awareness, and they became a very important part in the development of what Albert Thibaudet called "the republic of the book" in his classic 1936 essay, *Histoire de la litérature française de 1789 à nos jours.*[2] Books both represent and preserve cultural and institutional power. For hundreds of years, rulers and establishments had interests in keeping the common people away from books and from the knowledge included in and acquired by reading. Books were sequestered in private libraries owned by kings, wealthy nobles, and clerics, especially by the Catholic Church, where manuscripts were copied in monasteries and were considered to be the property of the pope. Books are not merely simple material objects. They are objects that offer symbolic powers and habits. Sociologist Pierre Bourdieu called the accessibility of books and what they represent "a privilege," a source of social hierarchy and power.[3]

From the earliest days of printing, Hebrew *musar* texts were printed and disseminated throughout the Jewish Diaspora. Although they were considered religious texts, they did not necessarily deal with Jewish law per se but served as leisurely reading matter that a pious man might peruse after his evening prayers or on the Sabbath.

In fact, *musar* books are still common reading material in Orthodox communities, even among women. Since the nineteenth century, some have even been modified to suit less-educated individuals and have also been adapted for children.[4] Hebrew *musar* texts have always been somewhat of a hybrid phenomenon. Initially, only well-educated Jews could understand them; nonetheless, Jews, in general, perceived them as being almost sacred, because they were written in the holy language of the Bible, yet dealt with everyday Jewish life and conduct. Regardless of whether or not they fully understood them, respectable and pious Jews kept Hebrew books, *musar* among them, in their homes.

In regard to the narratological aspect of these books, here they have been treated as literary art with particular literary features. The *musar* narrator has a special place in such texts, being the moderator between the ethical prose framework and the adapted, embedded folktales; it is the author who blends his didactic duty with literary pleasure.

The coming of print in the fifteenth century found Hebrew culture ready to adopt the new technology to circulate canonical Jewish writings and popular medieval texts to all the Jewish communities in the premodern world.[5] Print technology served as a catalyst for the development of an impressive Jewish book market and the Jewish "republic of the book." A large number of premodern texts emerged, which competed for acceptance by connoisseurs.[6] One of the most impressive phenomena of premodern Jewish culture was the flourishing of the *musar* literature, in all the Jewish languages. Throughout its history, this literature had consistently been one of the largest and most influential literary genres in Jewish culture.

Isaiah Tishby and Joseph Dan noted in their introduction to *Hebrew Musar Literature*:

> Musar literature should not be regarded as just one branch of the literature of religious philosophy—the branch of ethics—but also as an area of creativity that has a literary purpose of its own, whose aim is to impart literary pleasure together with knowledge. Whereas the literature of religious philosophy does not usually devote special attention to the form of its written essays, in Musar literature, the author directs his efforts to achieve perfection in both content and form.[7]

Tishby, Dan, and their followers consider the notion that there are immanent positivistic, formal, textual, artistic, linguistic, and structural principles in *musar* works that constitute its common denominator. On the other hand, in his *Openness and Insularity*, Elbaum devotes a chapter to *musar* literature, sermons, and homilies, in which he discusses different forms—all of which fit under the rubric of moral instruction.[8] What emerges from Elbaum's work is that *musar* literature is not so much a genre unto itself but rather a mode of thought adapted to existing genres. In support of this argument, he offers examples of moral values adapted to the literature of wills, conduct literature, moral instruction, and sermons.[9]

Emphasizing sociological factors, Avriel Bar-Levav argues that ethical literature is one of the means that religious culture uses to adapt to a changing reality.[10] He contends that the aim of *musar* literature is to help shape the religious personality of its readers. The need for this emanated from the recognition that the principal mechanisms of religious socialization—prayer and the Mishnah—had become insufficient for the task, as they no longer addressed the full gamut of Jewish life and they ignored certain existing Jewish communities. *Musar* works were created as tools for Jewish socialization, in a very deep sense, owing to the goal of practical involvement in profound aspects of the readers' personalities. Clearly, reading played a major role in this process; the People of the Book assign great power to books and book learning.

Musar literature and folklore are bound together in an intertextual interdependency; these ethical texts use folklore, cite folklore, and are, in fact, based on folklore. Evincing the same characteristics as folklore in many ways, *musar* literature has a textual metasystem that includes types and subtypes of literary phenomena. By reading *musar* literature as ethnic paradigms viewed from a folkloristic perspective, it becomes possible to question long-established assumptions and definitions and to reread these texts as intended by their authors *and* as received by their original readership. After setting aside preconceived notions that dismiss their potential as literature with poetic value that might stand for itself, it is easier to witness the aesthetic appeal and the literary diversity of the *musar* texts and to recognize the original, but freshly uncovered, set of criteria for better understanding them.

The premodern, scholarly *musar* authors said little or nothing in their paratexts about being storytellers or collectors and preservers of folktales.[11] They made no mention of the fact that they had incorporated oral and written narrative traditions and did not claim to be the gatekeepers and conveyers of those traditions. This entire idea of using folktales to enhance moral instruction was something that these premodern Jewish authors either tried to conceal or were not aware of; they make no acknowledgment of the contrasts between the overt content of the chapter and the content of the folktales embedded in them. Nor did they admit to modifying popular folktales, as they reframed them to fit into their *musar* works. With their didactic mindset and goals, they paid no attention to the literary novelty of this *musar* metasystem, nor did they assess its impact on literature and folklore, or its sociocultural reception in general.[12] Today, modern scholars have analytical and critical views extrinsic to the *musar* texts, whereas those premodern *musar* authors had pragmatic, and perhaps what we might call naïve, views intrinsic to their texts, such as concerns for the well-being of the readership. Table 4 summarizes the structure of the Hebrew musar text from a literary perspective.

Musar literature, this newly identified, mixed literary genre, revealed by means of a modern reading, applies, of course, to texts written, borrowed and adapted, and published not primarily as literary products but rather as didactic devices. The *musar* authors, most of whom were leaders in their communities (Orthodox rabbis, religious Jewish educators, and Jewish philosophers), did not see themselves as literary authors, but as purveyors of Jewish theological concepts, especially Jewish values. They were not attempting artistic creativity; on the contrary, they wrote about conventional themes and conformed to normative formats. However, they

Table 4: The Structure of a *Musar* Text

	Content	**Function**
Paratext	Author's prologue [optional]	Framing declaration
Component 1	Nonfictional, ethical prose	Moral guidance
Component 2	Folktale—literary prose	Literary metaphor
Paratext	Author's epilogue [optional]	Reframing declaration

did their best to introduce traditional ideas in novel ways and were very familiar with the expectations of their readership.

Premodern *musar* literature was not experimental; in fact, it was more like terra firma. It was not a question of producing new genres or even of being aware of existing ones. While the prologues and epilogues of the authors represent the internal Jewish ethical and sociocultural perspective, the genre classification per se embodies an external perspective—and those two views complement each other. This is admittedly anachronistic, since premodern thinking blurred many boundaries between categories that moderns find salient. However, the modern reframing illustrated in this book has the advantage of enabling the exploration of certain cultural phenomena found in the premodern *musar* literature from a political perspective, that is, reading the texts with an awareness of the struggling voices within; the politics, both of texts and of academic disciplines, are much clearer in retrospect. Obviously, both the premodern *musar* authors and readers of *musar* literature were bound by certain contemporary norms; the latter had clear expectations and enjoyed plots that conformed to familiar patterns.

As a twenty-first-century reader, the challenge was to classify the various embedded *musar* tales into delineated, meaningful categories. These categories have been conceived to serve as a systematic database for other books and other *musar* folktales, embedded in books that were not surveyed here.[13]

In the context of medieval and early modern Jewish culture, authors and readers were part of the same community. They respected the past and appreciated the ancient inheritance, and welcomed new, but not too new, texts. They trusted the familiar formats, had conservative tastes and expectations, and preferred to read either about the same characters in different plots or different characters in similar contexts. They were much more interested in the didactic, ethical content than in literary experimentation or literary pleasure as a purpose. They always attended to a theological or a social goal in preference to the aesthetic content.

By studying the *musar* tales, marvelous and diverse literary themes have been identified, involving many aspects of Jewish life and thought. The premodern *musar* authors straddled the thin line between literally putting the fear of God into their readers and offering them moral support. On one hand, they wanted to keep the attention of the readership on the ethical messages, but on the other hand, in order to enthrall them, here and there amid the somber texts they mixed in bits of the carnivalesque, some fantastic, grotesque, or lewd fiction, extreme or radical violence and adventure, to open readers' imaginations and pique their interests. Some of these tales portrayed the dark side of human existence, coupled with a shiny, bright future and the chance for redemption and salvation. It is likely that the sheer volume and popularity of such written *musar* texts and tales, along with the oral sermons they heard regularly in their synagogues, created a vast impact in Jewish communities the world over. In a sense, each *musar* text was also sort of a minianthology of folktales, which collectively influenced the readers.

By identifying this new corpus, the *musar* folktale, this book opens a new avenue for studying a highly influential literature. The corpus preserves many intriguing plots, whose function within a didactic context demands analysis. The tales are entertaining, though not intended for entertainment; they are humorous and worldly, though intended for serious and transcendent purposes. These indefatigable, powerful, timeless folktales enliven their didactic, sometimes somber, ethical prose contexts. They are ripe for future study.

Appendix 1

Musar Compilations Cited

The following chronological list, earliest to latest, provides the details of the selected Hebrew *musar* publications, their transliterated and translated English titles, their authors, and the first publication dates and publishers that served as the sources for the selected folktales found in this study.[1] Some of the texts are anonymous and some were translated into other Jewish languages or were printed simultaneously in Hebrew and other languages, but most of them have not yet been published in annotated, academic editions. Note that Hebrew *musar* texts consisting solely of nonfictional prose (that is, containing no folktales) were excluded from this research sample: *Orḥot haim* [The paths of life] by R. Asher b. Jeḥiel (ca. 1250–1327); *Tomer Devorah* [Deborah's palm tree][2] by R. Moses b. Jacob Cordovero (sixteenth century); and *Beḥinat 'olam* [The inspection of the world] by R. Jedaiah b. Abraham Bedersi (1270–1340). The following paragraphs introduce the *musar* texts that met the research criteria and were selected for this study.

The earliest publication selected, *Ḥovot ha-Levavot* [Duties of the hearts], was originally written in Judeo-Arabic by philosopher and rabbi Baḥya b. Joseph Ibn Paquda (Zaragoza, Spain, ca. 1050–1120). This work was later translated into Hebrew by Judah b. Saul Ibn Tibbon (Granada, 1120–ca. 1190) and was first published in Naples in 1490.[3] The book is divided into ten chapters, all devoted to the relationship between humanity and God: knowing God, having confidence in God, loving God, and so on. Ibn Paquda writes in his introduction that his sources of inspiration are Islamic mysticism, Islamic theology, and Christian writings. He does not specifically mention folktales as being of special interest, in spite of their inclusion.[4]

Tiqun Middot ha-Nefesh [Rectifying the moral qualities of the soul], written by the Andalusian poet, philosopher, and rabbi Solomon b. Judah Ibn Gabirol (Spain, 1021–70), was originally written in a Judeo-Arabic dialect and was later translated into Hebrew by Ibn Tibbon; the first print edition was published in Constantinople in 1550. It has five parts, based on the five senses, and each part is divided into chapters dealing with the vices and virtues associated with each sense. For example, pride, humility, mercy, and cruelty are associated with sight.[5] The text is written in a minimalistic style, and all the ideas presented regarding vices and virtues would later be developed by other authors. In spite of its minimalism, the text contains a group of folktales, later adopted by other authors as well. In his introduction, Ibn Gabirol wrote: "Seeing that most men are not sufficiently versed in the ruling of their qualities to enable them to regulate these according to ethical standards and a rational method (*'al derekh ha-musar veha-sēkhel*), we have resolved to write a satisfactory treatise concerning this, which shall contain an account *in extenso* of the qualities (*middot*), the ways in which to use them, and the mode in which to bring about their improvement."[6]

Ibn Gabirol declared that the purpose of his treatise was to help people adapt and improve their moral qualities based upon principles of ethics and logic. To that end, he included a description of the virtues and how best to apply them. In other words, he provided a pragmatic guide designed to influence individual behavior. He employed the word *musar* (Hebrew; *al-khlaq* in Arabic), which he associated with practical Jewish law (*halakhah*), and *middot* (measures or limits), which he defined as "the qualities that regulate and moderate human behavior." Ibn Gabirol made clear his pragmatic intent to bring about the emendation of human social conduct.

Mivḥar ha-Peninim [Selected pearls], ascribed also to Ibn Gabirol, was likewise written in a Judeo-Arabic dialect and translated into Hebrew by Ibn Tibbon. There is scholarly disagreement as to whether Ibn Gabirol actually composed this work, which features more than fifty sections and distinguishes the different types of vices and virtues.[7] Though similar in its minimalistic style to other works by Ibn Gabirol, *Mivḥar ha-Peninim* was compiled as a sequence of sayings and parables. It also exemplifies the influence of Muslim writings on Jewish literature in the medieval era and the cultural interactions that occurred in Muslim Spain.[8]

Sha'arē Teshuvah [The gates of repentance], by Spanish moralist, and rabbi Jonah b. Abraham Gerondi (Spain, 1200–1263), was first published in Constantinople in 1518. It is thought that this text was part of a larger *musar* work that was lost. It has four chapters, four "gates," each of which deals with a different aspect of repentance: the actions of repentance, the causes of repentance, good and evil behaviors, and the atonement for each offense.[9]

Ma'alot ha-Middot [The degrees of the virtues] was handwritten by Jeḥiel b. Jekuthiel Anaw (Rome, 1260–89), a famous scholar, poet, and cantor. It was published much later in Constantinople in 1512 under the title *Bēt middot* and subsequently published many times as *Ma'alot ha-Middot*; the first such version was the 1556 edition, printed in Cremona (located in Italy today) by Vicenzo Conti.[10] The title of this work suggests the image of a staircase or ladder, of a pious person reaching higher degrees of virtue. Jeḥiel Anaw was also a scribe, a copier of books, and his most famous work is his handwritten copy of the Jerusalem Talmud, now known as the "Leiden Manuscript" (Oriental 4720). *Ma'alot ha-Middot* has several adaptations and has been translated into other Jewish and non-Jewish languages. Its text influenced later *musar* authors, such as Isaac Aboab in his *Menorat ha-Ma'or*.[11]

Menorat ha-Ma'or [The seven-lamp of light],[12] written by R. Isaac b. Abraham Aboab (Spain, fl. 1300), a scholar and kabbalist, was first published in Constantinople in 1513 or 1514. It is divided into seven chapters, in line with the seven candles in the Jewish *menorah* (a "seven-lamp"), each chapter's title including the word *candle* to emphasize the idea of light. The title of his book refers to the light associated with pious life, while creating the metaphor of a lamp that lightens the house from the inside, just as its readers will gain light in their lives.[13]

In his introduction to *Menorat ha-Ma'or*, Aboab wrote of his hopes for his potential readership: "And they shall no longer go astray, like sheep without a shepherd." He further noted that he was deliberately trying to make his work appealing to the uneducated, offering "important and powerful words, sweet as honey, to fill the emptiness with knowledge." Nevertheless, Aboab sought to appeal to people at all levels (social and academic), affirming that his book would "be an aid to the great," while also "appealing to the simple . . . promising for beginners and a good introduction for those less able."[14]

Orḥot Ṣaddiqim [The ways of the righteous],[15] an anonymous text from Ashkenaz, was first published in Yiddish in Isny im Allgäu (a town located in today's Ravensbrück district in Germany) in 1542 and, in 1581, in Hebrew in Prague. It is divided into twenty-eight chapters, each devoted to a different vice or virtue—for example, silence, concern, agility, and other unusual topics for this kind of *musar* book. Its title suggests the metaphor of the road chosen by pious Jews. Its Hebrew edition contains a large group of folktales, some of them taken from the rabbinic literature, and others influenced by Muslim and Christian medieval works. The Ashkenazi background of this unknown author is evident in his attitudes toward hedonism and its contrary, asceticism, which are main issues of interest in this cultural context.[16]

Yesh Noḥalin [There are those who inherit], by noted talmudist Abraham b. Shabbetai Horowitz (Prague, 1540–1615), was written as an ethical will from a father to his sons and deals with taking the right path through life. Beyond the mere bequeathment of physical property, Jewish wills commonly served an ethical function,[17] delivering *musar* instruction, imparting parental tradition, and passing on the divine laws of good conduct. Later in his life, Horowitz joined the contemporary mystics residing in Prague, reflected in the symbolic nature of this text. When the first printed edition appeared in Prague in 1615, hardly any attention was paid to *Yesh Noḥalin* as a literary work in general nor as a *musar* text in particular. However, the simple and easily understandable folktales embedded in this ethical will offer a valuable contribution to the *musar* corpus studied here.

Ṣemaḥ ṣaddiq [Righteous growth], written by the Venetian poet, cantor, preacher, and rabbi Judah Aryeh or Leon of Modena (1571–1648), was first printed in Venice in 1600. It was an adaptation of a thirteenth-century

Italian moralistic book entitled *Fiore di Virtu* [Flower of virtue], written by Brother Tommaso Gozzadini (Bologne, 1260–1329). Besides the Hebrew rendition, it was also translated into many European vernaculars. This *musar* book has forty chapters, each devoted to a different vice or virtue—for example, cruelty, modesty, and generosity.

Qav ha-yashar [The just measure], by R. Zvi Hirsch Kaidanover (1648–1712), was first published in 1705 in Frankfurt am Main in both Yiddish and Hebrew, and the *Catalogue of the National Library of Israel* lists more than a hundred printed editions.[18] This *musar* book, which has 102 chapters, deals with all facets of mundane life, for example the education of children, the making of a good marriage, the value of reading, the value of friendship, and much more. On the title page of the 1706 Frankfurt am Main edition of *Qav ha-yashar*, Kaidanover wrote: "Small in quantity and great in quality, a fine book to benefit body and soul. Whoever reads it will be pure of heart and pure as the sun."[19] By asserting the connection between body and soul, Kaidanover maintained that his book could make a reader more honest and righteous. In the introduction, he described the contents as "words that sit well with the reader and draw his heart to listening to them."[20] That is, the explicit rhetorical purpose of the work was to engage the reader and thereby persuade him to correct his ways. At the same time, the words *musar* and *middot* are absent from the prologue, although each of its forty-two chapters revolves around moral qualities and virtues. Kaidanover elaborated on the mind-body connection, as well as on refinement of the spirit, resulting from the reading of ethical literature. Kaidanover's work aimed at calming the spirit and offering the public knowledge that it did not yet have: "I have written this book," he stated, "not to boast of it or be crowned with glory. . . . My only aim," he continued, "at my time of suffering and tribulation, is to bring respite to my soul and give merit to the many."

Shēveṭ Musar [The rod of morality], written by kabbalist, *dayyan* (a Jewish law judge), and preacher R. Elijah ha-Kohen ha-Itamari (Izmir, Turkey, 1659–1729), was first printed in Constantinople in 1712. It has fifty-two chapters, one for each week of the year. This notorious and horrific work was eventually translated into all the Jewish languages and appeared in dozens of printed editions. The introduction to the book was written in R. Elijah's voice:

> There is nothing great or small that I did not include in regard to the *musar* of man that subjugates the sinner's soul to bring it back to its Creator to dwell under the wings of the Divine Presence. [My aim was] to bring about corrections of transgressions from other writers or books, with the little wisdom that the Lord granted to me to understand that he who comes to purify is aided. I have written three essays that speak of repentance and in them are included several innovations. I have cited several articles on the subject of repentance, because he who engages in *musar* does penance, so that the reader will know how to repent and how to correct his ways and know the virtues of repentance and the advantages that accrue to him who repents.[21]

Mesillat Yesharim [The path of the upright], by the Italian poet, kabbalist, and philosopher R. Moshe Ḥaim Luzzatto (acronym *Ramḥal*, Padua, 1707–46), was first printed in Amsterdam in 1740. It has twenty-six chapters, each of which is devoted to a different aspect of embracing virtues as an expression of the love of God. This compilation is presented as a metaphorical ladder, which the reader is invited to climb as a spiritual journey, while reading chapter after chapter in turn. Each chapter represents a metaphorical step; for instance, "caution" and "agility" are found on a lower step than "humility" and "adherence." These chapters are called "steps" to a better way of life. The present research uses its latest text, published on the brink of the modern period of Hebrew literature.

Appendix 2

Additional *Musar* Tales

The Tefillin

THERE ONCE WAS a royal decree forbidding Jews to wear tefillin (phylacteries). There was a man named Elisha', whom they called Elisha', "the wing man," who got the name one day when he was wearing his phylacteries despite the royal decree. When a guard started running toward him, Elisha' tried to hide the phylacteries in his hand. When the guard approached Elisha', the guard asked: "What are you hiding in your hand?" And Elisha answered: "It's nothing, just the wings of a dove." And when Elisha' opened his hand, the phylacteries had transformed into a dove that flew away. From that day on, Elisha' was called "the wing man." (Kad ha-qemaḥ, chapter 1)

The Humble Sage

THERE ONCE WAS a king who said to a sage: "Whatever you ask of me, I can give you for all of your life." The sage replied: "Why would I take anything from you, for I am richer than you are?" The king was astonished and asked: "How is it possible for someone to be richer than I am?" And the sage answered: "Because I am happier with the little that I have than you are with the plenty that belongs to you." (Ma'alot ha-Middot, chapter 21)

Stones Outside Your Field

Once there was a farmer who cleared his field of stones by throwing them into the street. A pious man saw this and scolded him: "You fool, why are you throwing the stones onto your own property? True, the field is your property, but although the street belongs to the public, it is your property as well." And the pious man laughed at the farmer, since the latter did not understand this strange concept. Many days later, when the farmer was forced to sell his field, he had no choice but to walk in the street, where he stumbled on the very same stones that he had thrown there. And the farmer admitted that the pious man had been right. (Menorat ha-Ma'or, part 2, chapter 1, section 2)

The Praying Pious Man and the Bishop

Once there was a pious man praying on the road. A bishop who was passing by greeted the pious man, but the latter did not acknowledge him, since he was in the middle of his prayers, and he would not stop. After the pious man finished praying, the bishop asked him: "Isn't it written in your Bible that one should safeguard one's life? I should have cut your head off for your bad behavior." The pious man answered: "You are afraid of a flesh and blood ruler, but I fear God; if I do not pray, it is like cutting off my head." The bishop listened and allowed the pious man to return to his home in peace. (Menorat ha-Ma'or, part 3, chapter 3, section 1)

The Productive Field

Once there was a pious man who had a productive field that yielded a crop of a thousand units each year, out of which, according to Jewish law, he gave ten percent to the poor. When he was on his death bed, he asked that his son follow his example, and give as much charity as he could, so he would maintain the family's wealth. After the father passed away, his son did not abide by his father's wishes. In the first year, he gave ten percent, in the second year he gave a little less, in the third year still less, and so on. In the meantime, the yield of his field began to decrease, until he produced a crop only a hundred units, which had been what his father had given to charity regularly. As the son sat mourning his lost wealth, his relatives came to visit him, dressed as if coming to a celebration. The son said to them: "Are you here for a celebration? I am not celebrating; I am very sad. You should comfort me." The relatives answered: "Why shouldn't we be celebrating? Once, you were a landlord and God was the high priest, and now God has become the landlord of your property, and you are his high priest." Then, the son understood and gave generously to charity, as Jewish law decrees, and regained his wealth. (Menorat ha-Ma'or, part 3, chapter 7, section 2)

Drowning at Sea

ONCE, SOME FOUR HUNDRED BOYS AND GIRLS were taken as captives, with the intent to turn them into prostitutes. The children, who were aware of their intended fate, asked: "If we are drowned at sea, will we get to heaven?" And one of the older ones answered: "Yes, we will." When they heard his answer, they all jumped into the sea and drowned. (Menorat ha-Ma'or, part 5, chapter 3, section 2)

The Pregnant Woman and Her Mother

ONCE THERE WAS A pregnant woman who had a serious quarrel with her mother, so her mother was not near her when she went into labor. The pregnant woman was lying downstairs, and her mother was upstairs. Each time the pregnant woman screamed downstairs, her mother groaned upstairs. And the neighbors said to the mother: "What are you doing? Are you giving birth as well?" And the mother answered: "My girl is giving birth with great difficulty, and even though I'm not speaking to her, because she made me very angry, I can't help screaming with her. When my daughter's in trouble, then I'm in trouble, as well." (Menorat ha-Ma'or, part 3, chapter 3, section 1)

The Father Who Was Cursed

There once was a pious man who was arguing with another man at the city gate, near where the judges sat and received people. This pious father had come to the gate with his son, while another man was cursing and humiliating him with ugly words. The son got furious and wanted to hit the cursing man for his offensive behavior, but the pious father said to his son: "Let the man go, because, if he's right, then I deserve the curses, but if he's lying, why should I be angry, since God knows the truth." (Menorat ha-Ma'or, part 3, chapter 2, section 1)

The Gossip

Once a man came to his friend and told him that he would no longer be his friend. The friend asked the man: "Why have you decided to end our friendship?" The man answered: "Because I heard that people are saying bad things about you." And the friend asked: "Did you hear me saying bad things about other people?" The man said: "No, never." "If so," said the friend, "you should end your friendship with the gossips and not with me." (Mivḥar ha-Peninim, chapter 51)

The Innocent Man and His Wife

Once there was a king who ordered the execution of a wise man, although he was innocent, because the wise man would not lie. When the king's men were taking him to carry out his sentence, his wife cried. The doomed wise man asked her: "Why are you crying?" And she answered: "Because I know that you're innocent." And her husband said: "Would you prefer that I was sentenced for being guilty?" (Mivḥar ha-Peninim, chapter 4)

Pretending to Be Mute

Once there was a group of women sitting together and talking about the day of divine judgment and saying that everyone would have to give an account of their behavior throughout their whole life. And one of the women laughed and said: "When I come before the divine court and am asked about my behavior, I will pretend to be mute, so that I will not have to answer." Several days after she had said this, she became mute to her dying day. (Qav ha-yashar, chapter 1)

The Wrong Grave

Once there was a pious man who was buried among evil people. And every night he appeared in the dreams of his loved ones and demanded that his burial place be changed. He shouted and cried in their dreams, because he claimed that, since he had evil neighbors, he was not receiving the secrets of the Torah, so his soul was dry. His relatives were quite disturbed and, eventually, felt obliged to have him exhumed and reburied elsewhere. (Qav ha-yashar, chapter 6)

The Shining Pious Man

There once was a pious man who passed away. After his death, he came to his widow in a dream, and his hair and beard were shining like a flame. His wife asked him: "How come you deserve this shining fire in the other world?" And the pious husband answered: "Although I was pious and studied the Torah, what gave me the shining hair is that I did not talk about anything except for Torah and good deeds. God Himself is personally looking after people who talk little and are wholly concerned with the love of God." (Qav ha-yashar, chapter 12)

Elijah and the Bad Smell

THERE ONCE WAS a pious man who met the Prophet Elijah on the road. As they were walking together, they passed near the rotting corpse of an animal and the stench near it was so bad that the pious man had to cover his nose, but the Prophet Elijah was not bothered by the odor. Then they passed by a stranger, dressed like an honorable man, walking proudly on the road. Upon seeing him, the Prophet Elijah put his hand on his nose. The pious man asked the Prophet Elijah: "How come you were not bothered by the stench of the dead animal, but were bothered by the stranger?" Elijah answered: "If you go near an impure animal, you may be pure again a couple of hours later, but if you go near a person like that, the impurities inflicted on you will last much longer." (Qav ha-yashar, chapter 7)

The Disappointed Farmer

THERE ONCE WAS A FARMER who planted a vineyard. He dug up the ground and removed all the pebbles, planted the seedlings, and cut stones to build a winery and a watch tower, so that he could eat and drink there. He hoped that the grapes would grow well, but it turned out that all of them were rotten. When the farmer saw that all his work was for nothing, he got very angry. He took an ax and began to destroy everything that he had built, tearing down all the buildings and the fence, and his field began to grow wild with weeds. He did all this because he was expecting to enjoy himself but was disappointed. (Shēveṭ Musar, chapter 7, section 8)

The Child and the Wolf

ONCE THERE WAS A PIOUS MAN standing in prayer, when a wolf came along and took his young son; but the man would not stop praying, even though he saw that his child had been taken. After he finished praying, his students came and asked him: "Didn't you pity yourself when the wolf came and took your son?" And the pious man answered: "No, I did not." As he was answering, the wolf came back and put the child back in his place. Then the pious man asked the boy: "What did the wolf do to you?" And the boy answered: "The wolf took me to a ruined place, and I heard a voice telling him: 'This is not the right child; you took the child of a different man'." And, while the boy was telling his story, they all heard loud crying, and everyone was saying that another man's child had been bitten by a wolf. (Shēveṭ Musar, chapter 22, section 4)

The Son Saves His Father in the Afterlife

THERE ONCE WAS an evil man, who was sentenced to languish in Hell for the crimes he'd committed when he was alive. He left behind a son, who was just as evil. A pious man took the evil son and taught him Torah. At night, the evil man revealed himself to the pious man in his dreams, and told him: "You should know that, from the first day my son learned his first verse, my sentence was lightened. And since the day he learned the *Qri'at shma'* my sentence was reduced by a day, every day, since the sentence of evil people in Hell is reviewed seven times each day. When my son began to study Talmud, I was released from my punishment; and when they started to call him 'Rabbi', I was honored and given a seat with the pious in Heaven. Each day that he gains a new insight in his study, I receive honors in Heaven. God bless the one who leaves a scholarly son in this world." (Shēveṭ Musar, chapter 40, section 1)

Worries Destroy the Heart

ALEXANDER THE GREAT WAS TOLD by Aristotle, his teacher, that being worried causes the heart to be ruined, and he wanted to check if that was true. He took some cows—which are similar in their natures to human beings—and put them in a dark prison for many days. Then he had them fed and slaughtered. When he opened their corpses, he found out that their hearts were ruined, which is how he decided that Aristotle was right. (Tiqun Middot ha-Nefesh, chapter 8)

Three Friends

There once was a man who had three friends. He loved the first friend very much. He had less love for the second friend. And he did not love or appreciate the third friend at all. The king once sent his guards to arrest the man and bring him to the palace. He was frightened, because he thought that the king would kill him, so he decided to ask his beloved friend to accompany him to the palace and talk to the king on his behalf. But his beloved friend refused to come with him. Then, he went to ask the second friend for support; and the second friend said: "I will escort you all the way to the palace, but I will not go in with you." Then, the man went to the third friend, whom he did not like much at all. The third friend said: "I will escort you to the palace and go in with you, and the king will release you." The first friend is money, which the man loved, but after death, the money will not go to the afterlife with him. The second friend is his family, who will escort the man to his grave, but cannot go with him into the afterlife. The third friend is repentance and good deeds, which will accompany a man all his life, to his death, and into the afterlife. (Yesh Noḥalin, preface)

Notes

Introduction

1 All the titles of the Hebrew and Yiddish texts included in this book also appear with their translated English titles in the Index of *Musar* Texts and Primary Sources.

2 Micha Joseph Bin-Gorion [a.k.a. Berdyczewski or Berdichevsky], *Mi-Meqor Yisra'el* (Tel Aviv: Dvir, 1938), no. 274; Micha Joseph Bin Gorion, *Mimekor Yisrael: Classical Jewish Folktales*, abbr. and ann. edition, ed. Emanuel Bin Gorion, trans. Israel Meir Lask (Bloomington: Indiana University Press, 1990), no. 75, 149.

3 For more on the act of reading see Wolfgang Iser, "The Reading Process: A Phenomenological Approach," *New Literary History* 3, no. 2 (1972): 279–99; and Iser, *The Act of Reading: A Theory of Aesthetic Response* (Baltimore, MD: Johns Hopkins University Press, 1978).

4 This study is a continuation of an earlier discussion of folktales begun in printed Hebrew books, such as Vered Tohar, *The Book of Tales, Sermons and Legends (Ferrara 1554): An Anthology of Hebrew Stories from the Print Era* (Tel Aviv: Hakibbutz Hameuchad, 2016). See also one of the classic Hebrew essays on the general subject: Joseph Dan, "Ethical Literature," in *Encyclopaedia Judaica* 6 (1972): 922–32.

5 This issue was discussed by Zeev Gries, *The Book in the Jewish World, 1700–1900*, rev. ed. (Oxford: Littman Library of Jewish Civilization, 2010). See also, Tony Davenport, *Medieval Narrative* (Oxford: Oxford University Press, 2004); and also Malachi Beit-Arie, "The Relationship between Early Hebrew Printing and Handwritten Books: Attachment or Detachment?" [in Hebrew], *Scripta Hierosolymitana* 29 (1989): 1–26.

6 See Jacob Elbaum, *Openness and Insularity: Late Sixteenth Century Jewish Literature in Poland and Ashkenaz* [in Hebrew] (Jerusalem: Magnes Press, 1990).

7 This line of thought was inspired by the work of Eli Yassif: see "The Hebrew Narrative Anthology in the Middle Ages," *Prooftexts* 17, no. 2 (1997): 153–75, and *The Hebrew Folktale: History, Genre, Meaning* (Bloomington: Indiana University Press, 1999); and also Dan Ben-Amos, ed., *Folklore Genres* (Austin: University of Texas Press, 1976).

8 The present book was inspired by the idea of context as a major variable in the reading of folktales, as suggested by Dan Ben-Amos, "'Context' in Context," *Western Folklore* 52, no. 2/4 (1993): 209–26; Ben-Amos, "Jewish Studies and Jewish Folklore," *Proceedings of the World Congress of Jewish Studies, Division D* (1989): 1–20; and also Ben-Amos, *Ha-sifrut ha-'amamit ha-Yehudit* [Jewish folk literature] (Jerusalem: Magnes, 2006).

9 This main paradigm was coined in folklore studies by Alan Dundes, "From Etic to Emic Units in the Structural Study of Folktales," *Journal of American Folklore* 75 (1962): 95–105. See also Marvin Harris, "History and Significance of the Emic/Etic Distinction," *Annual Review of Anthropology* 5 (1976): 329–50. Also see Pavel Thomas, "Literary Genres as Norms and Good Habits," *New Literary History* 34, no. 2 (2003): 201–10.

10 For the definition and meaning of the term "habitus," see Pierre Bourdieu, *Outline of a Theory of Practice*, trans. Richard Nice (Cambridge: Cambridge University Press, 1977), 78–79.

11 For more, see Moses Gaster, *The Exempla of the Rabbis* (New York: Ktav, 1968).

Chapter 1

1 See Rosamond McKitterick, ed., *The Uses of Literacy in Early Mediaeval Europe* (Cambridge: Cambridge University Press, 1990).

2 Joseph Dan, *Ethical and Homiletical Literature* [in Hebrew] (Jerusalem: Keter, 1975).

3 One can see a mutual textual phenomenon in the rabbinic literature; see, e.g., Galit Hasan-Rokem, *Tales of a Neighbourhood: Jewish Narrative Dialogue in Late Antiquity* (Berkeley: University of California Press, 2003); Dina Stein, *Maxims, Magic, Myth: A Folkloristic Perspective of Pirkē de Rabbi Eli'ezer* [in Hebrew] (Jerusalem: Magnes Press, 2004). For another folkloristic approach, see also David Rotman, *Dragons, Demons and Wonderous Realms: The Marvelous in Medieval Hebrew Narrative* [in Hebrew] (Be'er-Sheva: Kinneret, Zmora-Bitan, Dvir and Heksherim Institute, Ben-Gurion University of the Negev, 2016).

4 b. Talmud, *Baba Batra* 8b—"Yesh Noḥalin."

5 For modern adaptations of and annotations of this story, see Micha Joseph Bin Gorion, *Mimekor Yisrael: Classical Jewish Folktales*, abbr. and ann.

edition, ed. Emanuel Bin Gorion, trans. Israel Meir Lask (Bloomington: Indiana University Press, 1990), no. 778 and no. 261, p. 478, respectively.

6 See b. Talmud, *Ta'anit* 21a. See also Hana Hendler, "Nachum of Gamzu and His Errand to King Caesar," in *Encyclopedia of the Jewish Story: Sippur Okev Sippur*, vol. 1., ed. Yoav Elstein, Avidov Lipsker, and Rella Kushelevsky (Ramat-Gan: Bar-Ilan University Press, 2004), 247–60.

7 Simon J. Bronner, "Folk Logic: Interpretation and Explanation in Folkloristics," *Western Folklore* 65, no. 4 (2006): 401–33.

8 See Haya Bar-Itzhak and Idit Pintel-Ginsberg, eds., *The Power of the Tale: The Jubilee Book of IFA, Israel Folklore Archive* [in Hebrew] (Haifa: Haifa University Press, 2008). It is beyond the scope of this study; however, many of the Hebrew folktales studied here may also be found in printed Jewish *musar* literature in languages such as Yiddish, and later, Ladino. Some books were translated from Hebrew to Yiddish immediately after their publication, while others were originally dual-language versions; nonetheless, a number of *musar* works were published only in Yiddish or only in Hebrew. For example, see Noga Rubin, *Conqueror of Hearts: Sefer Lev Ṭov by R. Isaac Ben Eliakim of Posen (Prague, 1620): A Central Ethical Book in Yiddish* [in Hebrew] (Tel Aviv: Hakibbutz Hameuchad, 2013). Though other Jewish languages have their places in Jewish culture, especially after the printing revolution, Hebrew has always been dominant and its presence throughout Jewish history symbolizes the Jewish essence. For more, see Chone Shmeruk, *Chapters in Yiddish Literature* [in Hebrew] (Tel Aviv: Tel Aviv University Press, 1978); Shmeruk, *Yiddish Literature in Poland* [in Hebrew] (Jerusalem: Magnes Press, 1981).

I should perhaps point out that my discussion on *musar* literature does not deal with the fine distinctions between the various eastern and western Jewish communities, nor does it explore the small details of different linguistic registers, because, in this research, I am creating an access road into these texts through a multicultural, structuralist prism, and primarily I am trying to focus the discussion on the matters of the methodology behind the creation of my innovative research corpus and its criticism.

9 Ryan Szpiech, *Conversation and Narrative: Reading and Religious Authority in Medieval Polemic* (Philadelphia: University of Pennsylvania Press, 2012), 61–90. For the classic research on the book, see Victor Tolan, *Petrus Alfonsi and His Medieval Readers* (Gainesville: University Press of Florida, 1993). For comparative research on the book, see Haim Schwarzbaum, *International Folklore Motifs in Petrus Alfonsi's "Disciplina Clericalis"* (Madrid: Talleres Graficos, 1961–1963). For a modern edition, see also Eberhard Hermes, ed., *The Disciplina Clericalis of Petrus Alfonsi* (Berkeley: University of California Press, 1977). Last but not least, see Dan Ben-Amos, *Ha-sifrut ha-'amamit ha-Yehudit* [Jewish folk literature] (Jerusalem: Magnes, 2006, 74–75), and his article in English, "Jewish Folk Literature," *Oral Tradition* 14, no. 1 (1999): 140–274.

10 See also the many shades of the current research on this work: Gabriel Ford, "Sociality at the Margins in Petrus Alfonsi's *Disciplina Clericalis*," *Digital Philology: A Journal of Medieval Cultures* 9 no. 1 (2020): 27–46, and his "Framing, Parataxis, and the Poetics of Exemplarity in Petrus Alfonsi's *Disciplina Clericalis*," *Medieval Encounters* 21, no. 1 (Jan. 2015): 26–49. See also Oscar Abenojar Sanjuan, "On the Sources of the Exemplum XXIII of the *Disciplina Clericalis* and Its Survival in the Iberian and Latin American Traditions," *Hispanofilia* 193 (Jan. 2021): 165–79.

11 See the scientific edition: Charles Swan, *Gesta Romanorum* (London: G. Bell & Sons, 1905). See also a newly updated translation into English by Christopher Stace, *Gesta Romanorum: A New Translation* (Manchester: Manchester University Press, 2016).

12 Eli Yassif, *The Hebrew Folktale: History, Genre, Meaning* (Bloomington: Indiana University Press, 1994), 120–32.

13 Here is a limited list: Albrecht Classen, "Alcohol, Drunkenness, and Excess—Consumption and Transgression in European Medieval and Early Modern Literature," *Neophilologus: An International Journal of Modern and Medieval Language and Literature* (July 2022): 1–22; Jennifer Alberghini, "Knowing Nature: Bear-Human Bestiality in the *Gesta Romanorum*," *Folklore* 132, no. 2 (2021): 189–207; Classen, "From the *Gesta Romanorum* to Werner Bergengruen: Literary Mirrors for Princes from the Late Middle Ages to the Twentieth Century," *Amsterdamer Beiträge zur Älteren Germanistik* 81, no. 1 (2021): 98–123. Friedrich, Udo, "Zur Verdinglichung der Werte in den *Gesta Romanorum*," n *Dingkulturen: Objekte in Literatur, Kunst und Gesellschaft der Vormoderne*, ed. Anna Mühlherr, Heike Sahm, Monika Schausten, and Bruno Quast, 249–66 (Berlin: Walter de Gruyter, 2016); Clark Colahan, "Episodes in Persiles and Sigismunda Shaped by 'Byzantine tales' from the *Gesta Romanorum*," *Hipogrifo* 3, no. 1 (2015): 129–39.

14 For more on this see the pioneering research of Rella Kushelevsky, who compared four handwritten versions of the *Midrash 'Aseret ha-Dibrot'* from the Ashkenazic domain, by especially focusing on the characteristics of the Parma Manuscript version, Parma 2269. See Kushelevsky, "*Midrash 'Aseret ha-Dibrot'* in MS Parma 2269," *Jerusalem Studies in Jewish Folklore* 29 (2015): 33–77, and her *Penalty and Temptation: Hebrew Tales in Ashkenaz, MS Parma 2295 (de-Rossi 563)* (Magnes: Jerusalem, 2010).

15 Nissim b. Jacob ibn Shāhīn, *An Elegant Composition Concerning Relief after Adversity: An Eleventh-Century Book of Comfort*, trans. William M. Brinner (New Haven, CT: Yale University Press, 1977).

16 The Harkavy manuscript, apparently copied in Egypt in the fourteenth to fifteenth centuries, may be seen in Julian Obermann, ed., *The Arabic Original of Ibn Shâhîn's Book of Comfort Known as the Ḥibbûr Yaphê of R. Nissîm b. Ya'aqobh* (New Haven, CT: Yale University Press, 1933).

17 The Rome Casanatense manuscript 3097 was written in Italian in 1428. The Paris manuscript 716 from Provence was written in Spanish and dated fourteenth to fifteenth centuries. The Warsaw manuscript 347 was written in Italian and is also dated in the fourteenth to fifteenth centuries.

18 The Hebrew edition of the text is that of Haim Ze'ev Hirschberg, *Ḥibbur Yafeh meha-Yeshu'ah* (Jerusalem: Rav Kook Talmudical Research Institute, 1954). Hirschberg translated the Harkavy manuscript into Hebrew, adding introductions and comments. See also Shraga Abramson, comp., *R. Nissim Ga'on: Ḥamishah sfarim: Sridim mey-hibburav yots'im la-or 'al pi kitvey yad* [R. Nissim Gaon: Five books: Remnants of essays published as manuscripts] (Jerusalem: Mekitse Nirdamim, 1965); Galit Brin, "Hebetim beyn tarbutiyim be-'Hibbur Yafe mena-Yeshuah'" [Inter-cultural aspects in "Hibbur yafe mena-Yeshuah"—Genre, thematics, and editorial trends], PhD diss., Bar-Ilan University, 2017.

19 The Oxford-Bodleian manuscript, Bodl. Or. 135, no. 1466, in the Neubauer Catalogue. The collection itself is pp. 300A–339B.

20 See Tohar, "Does Print Matter? The 16th Century Printed Editions of the Hebrew Essay 'Midrash on the Ten Commandments'," in *Aliento*, 10 (2018): 413–26. See also Eli Yassif, *Ke-Margalit ba-Mishbetset: Kovets ha-Sippurim ha-'Ivri bi-Yemey ha-Beynayim* (*Like a Pearl in a Slot: A Collection of the Hebrew Tales in the Middle Ages*). Tel Aviv: ha-Kibbutz ha-Me'uḥad, 2004.

21 Rella Kushelevsky, *Tales in Context: Sefer ha-Ma'asim in Medieval Northern France* (Detroit, MI: Wayne State University Press, 2017).

22 For the sake of brevity, each category is exemplified in the list by a single text.

23 Possibly adapted from al-Tanūkhī's (939–94 CE, Basra, Iraq) compilation of Arabic folktales, *Al-faraj ba'd al-shiddah* [The salvation after the hardship].

24 Usually pronounced in Yiddish as one word, *Ṣenerene*, or two, *Ṣeno Reno*—depending on the Yiddish dialect.

25 Here, a distinction should be made between literal explanations and homiletic explanations when classifying works as ethical texts.

26 Ze'ev Gries, *Conduct Literature (Regimen Vitae): Its History and Place in the Life of Beshṭian Ḥasidism* [in Hebrew] (Jerusalem: Bialik Institute, 1989), 1–40; Gries, *The Book as an Agent of Culture, 1700–1900* [in Hebrew]

(Tel Aviv: Hakibbutz Hameuchad, 2002), 57–64; for a partial English translation, see his, *The Book in the Jewish World, 1700–1900* (Oxford: Littman Library of Jewish Civilization, 2007). See also Micha Perry, *Tradition and Transformation: Knowledge Transmission among European Jews in the Middle Ages* [in Hebrew] (Tel Aviv: Hakibbutz Hameuchad, 2010). Also see Harris Bor, "Enlightenment, Values, Jewish Ethics: The Haskala's Transformation of the Traditional Musar Genre," in *New Perspectives on Haskalah*, ed. Shmuel Feiner and Dov Sorkin (London: Littman Library of Jewish Civilization, 2001), 48–63.

27 This notion rests, for example, on the very solid ground of the Christian culture of vices and virtues, which was firmly established in theological thought and practice in the medieval era; it was also based on handwritten manuscripts and printed books. See, e.g., Adolf Katzenellenbogen, *Allegories of the Virtues and Vices in Medieval Art: From Early Christian Times to the Thirteenth Century*, trans. Alan J. Crick (New York: Norton Library, 1964). See also Richard Newhauser, *The Treatise on Vices and Virtues in Latin and the Vernacular* (Turnhout, Bel.: Brepols, 1993). Also see Rosalind Hursthouse, *On Virtue Ethics* (Oxford: Oxford University Press, 2010). This notion is also a sequel of Muslim culture; see Charles E. Butterworth, "Medieval Islamic Philosophy and the Virtue of Ethics," *Arabica* 34, no. 2 (1987): 221–50; Mona Siddiqui, *The Good Muslim: Reflections on Classical Islamic Law and Theology* (Cambridge: Cambridge University Press, 2021).

28 Cordelia Hess, *Social Imagery in Middle Low German: Didactic Literature and Metaphorical Representation (1470–1517)* (Leiden, Neth.: Brill, 2013). Warner Berthoff, *Literature and the Continuances of Virtue* (Princeton, NJ: Princeton University Press, 2014); Jerome S. Bruner, *Relevance of Education* (New York: Norton Library, 1973).

29 Eli Yassif, *Book of Memories: Chronicles of Yeraḥme'el* [In Hebrew] (Tel Aviv: Tel Aviv University Press, 2001). For his aforementioned article see *Jerusalem Studies in Hebrew Literature* 9 (1986): 357–73 [in Hebrew]. See also Moses Gaster, trans., *Ha-Levi, Elazar ben Asher: The Chronicles of Jerahmeel* (New York: Ktav, 1971).

30 Bin Gorion, *Mimekor Yisrael.*

31 Kushelevsky, *Tales in Context.*

32 See, for example, the works of Sara Zfatman, Yassif, Kushelevsky, Ben-Amos, Schwarzbaum, and others, who took important steps in the interpretation and evaluation of medieval Hebrew stories found in folktale anthologies not within the *musar* literature: Sara Zfatman, *Between Ashkenaz and Sepharad: The Jewish Tale in the Middle Ages* [in Hebrew] (Jerusalem: Magnes Press, 1993); Yassif, "The Hebrew Narrative Anthology in the Middle Ages," *Prooftexts* 17, no. 2 (1997) and his *Hebrew Folktale*; Kushelevsky, *Penalty and Temptation*, and her *Midrash 'Aseret ha-Dibrot'*; Joseph Dan, *The Hebrew Story in the Middle Ages: Studies of Its History* [in Hebrew] (Jerusalem: Keter, 1974); and Ḥaim Schwarzbaum, *The Mishlē Shu'alim (Fox Fables) of Rabbi Berechiah ha-Nakdan: A Study in Comparative Folklore and Fable Lore* (Kiron, Isr.: Institute for Jewish and Arab Folklore Research, 1979).

33 As noted in Joseph Dan's "Ethical Literature," in *Encyclopaedia Judaica* 6 (1972), his *Hebrew Ethical and Homiletical Literature*; and also in his *On Sanctity: Religion, Ethics and Mysticism in Judaism and Other Religions* [in Hebrew] (Jerusalem: Magnes Press, 1998); as well as in Gries, *Book in the Jewish World*; and Gries, *The Hebrew Book: An Outline of Its History* [In Hebrew] (Jerusalem: Bialik Institute, 2015).

34 For instance, see Noga Rubin, "*Sefer Lev Ṭov* (Prague, 1620): The First Edition of the Book?" *Zuṭot* 5, no. 1 (2008): 121–27. Rubin and Zelda Kahan Newman, "Pious Wrappings, Troubling Insides," *Journal of Modern Jewish Studies* 7, no. 3 (2008): 269–82. For more on the attitude toward the individual experience: Peter Singer, *Applied Ethics* (Oxford: Oxford University Press, 1986).

35 See Alan Dundes, ed., *The Study of Folklore* (Englewood Cliffs, NJ: Prentice-Hall, 1964), and his "From Etic to Emic Units in the Structural Study of Folktales," *Journal of American Folklore* 75 (1962).

36 See Herbert Spencer, *On Social Evolution: Selected Writings*, ed. J. D. Peel (Chicago: University of Chicago Press, 1972); Elizabeth L. Eisenstein, *The Printing Press as an Agent of Change: Communication and Cultural Transformations in Early-Modern Europe* (Cambridge: Cambridge University Press, 1979); Robert Houston, *Literacy in Early Modern Europe: Culture and Education, 1500–1800* (London: Longman, 1988); McKitterick, ed., *The Uses of Literacy in Early Mediaeval Europe* (Cambridge: Cambridge University Press, 1992); Walter J. Ong, *Orality and Literacy: The Technologizing of the World* (New York: Routledge, 2012).

37 Shmuel Werses, "Studies on the Musar Literature of the Jews in Spain from the Early 13th Century until the Late 15th Century" [in Hebrew] (PhD diss., Hebrew University of Jerusalem, 1947).

38 Belsey, Catharine, "Problems of Literary Theory: The Problem of Meaning," *New Literary History* 14, no. 1 (1982): 175–82.

39 The *ATU* devotes a chapter to "The Foolish Wife and Her Husband," *ATU* 1380–*ATU* 1404. Sometimes brides behave like fools to get rid of unwanted husbands.

Chapter 2

1 See Ilaria Briata, "Repentance through Fear: Cosmic and Body Horror in *Shēveṭ Musar*," *European Journal of Jewish Studies* (*EJJS*) 14, no. 2 (2020): 264–84; and Jonathan Garb, "From Fear to Awe in Luzzatto's *Mesillat Yesharim*," *EJJS* 14, no. 2 (2020): 285–99.

2 Sigmund Freud, "The Dissolution of the Oedipus Complex," in *On Sexuality: Three Essays on the Theory of Sexuality and Other Works* (London: Penguin, 1991), 313–22.

3 Solomon Buber, *Midrash Tanḥuma* (Vilna: Romm Press, 1885), appendix to paragraph 1 [in Hebrew].

4 For a comprehensive review of the story and its different forms and sources, see Avidov Lipsker, "*Matya ben Ḥeresh*" [in Hebrew], in *Encyclopedia of the Jewish Story: Sippur Okev Sippur*, vol. 2, ed. Yoav Elstein, Avidov Lipsker, and Rella Kushelevsky, 275–90 (Ramat-Gan: Bar-Ilan University, 2009), 275–90.

5 Jean Paul Sartre, "The Look" in *Being and Nothingness: A Phenomenological Essay on Ontology*, trans. Hazel E. Barnes (New York: Washington Square Press, 1992), 340–400.

6 Rashi is the acronym for R. Shlomo Yiṣḥaqi (1040–1105), who lived in Troyes, France, and wrote the most famous commentary on the Hebrew Bible and a comprehensive commentary on the Talmud.

7 Appears in chapter 21 of the tenth century compilation, first printed as *Tanna devē Eliyahu* [in Hebrew] (Venice, 1598) and in a later Hebrew edition (Vienna: Ish Shalom, 1899). An English translation may be found in Rabbi Avraham Yaakov Finkel's *Tanna devē Eliyahu: Teachings from Eliyahu Hanavi* (Scranton, PA: Yeshivath Beth Moshe, 2013).

8 Collins, Terry, "Intimations of Feminism in Ancient Athens: Euripides' Medea," *Sydney Studies in English* 26 (2000): 3–24.

9 Nitza Abarbanel, *Eve and Lilith* [in Hebrew] (Ramat-Gan: Bar-Ilan University Press, 1994).

10 See motif no. B 29.1 "Face of Woman, Body of Serpent," in the Stith Thompson (ST) *Motif Index of Folk Literature* (Bloomington: Indiana University Press, 1966).

11 Compare with *Shulḥan Arukh, Yoreh De'ah, Laws of Excommunication and Bans*, section 334, which sharpens the distinction between excommunication and banning. I am grateful to Dr. Moshe Shushan for this reference. For an English version see online at Shulchan Aruch/Yoreh Deah/334—Wikisource (accessed Jan. 19, 2022) https://en.wikisource.org/wiki/Translation:Shulchan_Aruch/Yoreh_Deah/334.

12 Judah Feliks, "Dog," in *Encyclopaedia Judaica*, 2nd ed., vol. 5, ed. Michael Berenbaum and Fred Skolnik (Jerusalem: Macmillan Reference, 2007), 733.

13 R. Isaac b. Solomon Luria Ashkenazi (1534–72, Safed) was a Jewish mystic, a.k.a. *ha-Ari ha-Qadosh* [the Sacred Lion].

14 See *Merriam Webster Dictionary*, accessed Jan. 15, 2022, s.v. "bitch," www.merriam-webster.com/dictionary/bitch; and Gary Martin, *The Phrase Finder*, accessed Jan. 15, 2022, s.v. "son of a bitch," www.phrases.org.uk/meanings/son-of-a-bitch.html.

15 Maria Leach, ed., *Standard Dictionary of Folklore, Mythology and Legend*, vol. 1 (New York: Funk & Wagnalls, 1949), 319.

16 Leach, *Standard Dictionary of Folklore*.

17 Leach, *Standard Dictionary of Folklore*.

18 Erich Neumann, *The Great Mother: An Analysis of the Archetype*, trans. Ralph Manheim, 2nd ed., (Princeton, NJ: Princeton University Press, 1974).

19 Harold Walter Bailey, "'Bisclavret' in Marie de France," *Cambridge Medieval Celtic Studies* 1 (1981): 95–97; Matilde Tomaryn Bruckner, "Of Men and Beasts in 'Bisclavret'," *The Romanic Review* 82 (1991): 251–69; Tovi Bibring, "In *Ictu Oculi*: Reflections on Wolf and Beast by Berechia ha-Naqdan in the Context of Its Contemporary Versions," *Comparative Literature Studies* 56, no. 2 (2019): 374–401. For more on rabbinic thought about beasts and bestiality, see Jacob Neusner, "Bestiary, Rabbinic" in *Encyclopaedia of Judaism*, Brill Online Reference Works, accessed Feb. 10, 2022, https://referenceworks.brillonline.com/entries/encyclopaedia-of-judaism/bestiary-rabbinic-COM_0017?s.num=0.

20 From the 11th century.

21 This story was widespread in the Jewish narrative tradition of the Middle Ages. See, e.g., MS Parma, Palatina (de-Rossi 563) fols. 129b–130a (Northern France, late thirteenth century); MS Wolfenbüttel 36.25, *Midrash 'Aseret ha-Dibrot', Seventh Commandment* [18]–[19] (Ashkenazi script, fourteenth century); MS Paris, Bibliotheque Nationale de France (BNF), Heb. 716, *Ḥibbur Yafeh meha-Yeshu'ah*, R. Nissim of Qairouan, fols. 194b–195a, Provence (Sephardic script, fourteenth–fifteenth centuries); MS Paris, BNF, Heb. 716, fols. 222–23b, *Midrash 'Aseret ha-Dibrot'*, Provence (Sephardic script, fourteenth to fifteenth centuries); MS Rome, Contensa 3097, *Ḥibbur Yafeh*, fols. 100a–100b, rev. 107, fols. 173a–173b. Also, *Midrash 'Aseret ha-Dibrot'* (Provence script, 1438); MS Parma, Palatina, 2269 (de-Rossi 473) fols. 71a–71b; *Ḥibbur Yafeh*, MS Harkavy, in *The Arabic Original of Ibn Shâhîn's Book of Comfort Known as the Ḥibbûr Yaphê of R. Nissîm b. Ya'aqobh* (Judeo-Arabic, Egypt, fifteenth century), ed. Julian Obermann (New Haven, CT: Yale University Press, 1933), 120–23; MS New Haven, Yale University, Heb. 6, unpaginated (Kurdistan, 1540); *Ma'aseh bukh* (Basel, 1601/2), 80a–80b, par. 140 (Yiddish, 1602). Also see Vered Tohar,

"Rabbi Meir and His Friend's Wife," in *Encyclopedia of the Jewish Story*, vol. 3 (2013), 155–80.

22 On tests of truthfulness in folktales, see Aliza Shenhar, *From a Folktale to a Children's Tale* [in Hebrew] (Haifa: University of Haifa Press, 1982), 49–51.

23 For more on lions, see Revital Refael-Vivante, "Of Lions and Foxes: Power and Rule in Hebrew Medieval Fables," *Revista de Paz y Conflictos* 2 (2009), 24–43.

24 Dominic Peter Rotunda, *Motif Index of the Italian Novella in Prose* (Bloomington: Indiana University Press, 1942).

25 Robert Darnton, The Great Cat Massacre and Other Episodes in French Cultural History (New York: Basic Books, 1984).

26 Also echoing the words of Nitai ha-Arbeili in *Pirqē Avot* 1:7: "Distance yourself from an evil neighbor."

Chapter 3

1 For more on the "carnival sense of the world" and its effects in literature, see Mikhail Bakhtin, *Problems of Dostoevsky's Poetics*, ed. Caryl Emerson (Minneapolis: University of Minnesota Press, 1984) and his *Speech Genres and Other Late Essays*, trans. V. W. McGee (Austin: Texas University Press, 1986).

2 See Andrew Leslie, "How Stories Argue: The Deep Roots of Storytelling in Political Rhetoric," *Storytelling, Self, Society* 11, no. 1 (2015): 66–84.

3 Avraham Shaanan, *Dictionary of Modern Literature* [in Hebrew] (Tel Aviv: Yavne Publishing House, 1978), 1057–58. See also Jan Hokenson, *The Idea of Comedy: History, Theory, Critique* (Madison, NJ: Fairleigh Dickinson University Press, 2006); William Moelwyn Merchant, *Comedy: The Critical Idiom* (London: Methuen, 1972); Erich Segal, *The Death of Comedy* (Cambridge, MA: Harvard University Press, 2001).

4 Shaanan, *Dictionary of Modern Literature*, 1058.

5 Gilbert Murray, "Excurses on the Ritual Forms Preserved in Greek Tragedy," in *Themis: A Study of Social Origins of Greek Religion*, ed. Jane Harrison (Cambridge: Cambridge University Press, 1912), 341–63; Francis Macdonald Cornford, *The Origin of Attic Comedy* (London: Edward Arnold, 1914).

6 Not human marriage, but the union of the Earth Mother and the Heavenly Father: See Eli Rozik, *The Roots of Theatre: Rethinking Ritual and Other Theories of Origin* (Iowa City: University of Iowa Press, 2002), 49–68. See also Dana F. Sutton, *The Catharsis of Comedy* (Lanham, MD: Rowman & Littlefield, 1994); David J. Palmer, ed., *Comedy: Developments in Criticism* (Basingstoke, UK: Macmillan, 1984).

7 Rozik, *Roots of Theatre*, 49–68; Andreas Willi, "The Language of Greek Comedy: Introduction and Bibliographical Sketch," in *The Language of Greek Comedy*, ed. Andreas Willi (Oxford: Oxford University Press, 2002), 1–32.

8 Edward Quinn, *A Dictionary of Literary and Thematic Terms*, 2nd ed. (New York: Facts on File, 2006), 85–88. See also Robert Corrigan, *Comedy: Meaning and Form* (New York: Harper & Row, 1965); Northrop Frye, *Anatomy of Criticism* (Princeton, NJ: Princeton University Press, 1957); Harry Levin, *Playboys and Killjoys: An Essay on the Theory and Practice of Comedy* (New York: Oxford University Press, 1987).

9 Peter Childs and Roger Fowler, *The Routledge Dictionary of Literary Terms*, rev. ed. (London: Routledge, 1987), 28. See also John A. Cuddon, *A Dictionary of Literary Terms and Literary Theory*, 5th ed. (Chichester, UK: Wiley, 2013).

10 Cuddon, *Dictionary of Literary Terms*, 29.

11 Monika Fludernik, *An Introduction to Narratology*, trans. Patricia Hausler and Monika Fludernik (London: Routledge, 2009), 29–30; Shlomith Rimmon-Kenan, *Narrative Fiction: Contemporary Poetics* (London: Methuen, 1983).

12 For further references on this theme, see Julius Preuss, *Biblical and Talmudic Medicine*, trans. and ed. Fred Rosner (Northvale, NJ: Jason Aronson, 1993).

13 Hesiod's Greek poem "Theogony" was originally written ca. 700 BCE; in English translation, M. L. West, *Theogony and Works and Days* (Oxford: Oxford University Press, 1988), 14, lines 462–96.

14 Plutarch's original Greek biographical anthology, *Parallel Lives*, was written during the first century BCE; a complete English translation of chapters 2–10, initially translated by John Dryden and later revised by Arthur Hugh Clough, may be found online: *Plutarch: Lives of the Noble Grecians and Romans*, Gutenberg Project (1996), accessed Jan. 22, 2022, www.gutenberg.org.

15 See *The Kybalion: A Study of the Hermetic Philosophy of Ancient Egypt and Greece*, trans. William Walker Atkinson [pseud. "Three Initiates"] (Chicago: Yogi Publication Society, 1908), which states that everything has its own masculine and feminine principles.

16 Robert Fitzgerald, *Homer: The Odyssey* (New York: Vintage Books, 1990).

17 Eli Yassif, "The Exemplary Story in *Sefer Ḥasidim*," *Tarbiṣ* (1988): 220–23.

18 *Rut Zuṭa* is a *midrash aggadah* (a rabbinical, ethical, narrative commentary) of the Hebrew biblical book of Ruth, compiled during the tenth century. For a literary survey of the original text, see Ronit Shoshany, "A Study of Two Legends in *Midrash Ruth Zuṭa* in Light of *Ḥibbur Yafeh meha-Yeshu'ah*," *Jewish Studies: The Internet Journal* 7 (2008): 81–103, (accessed Feb. 9, 2022), jewish-faculty.biu.ac.il/en/node/1053.

19 *Yalquṭ Shim'oni* [Simon's anthology] is a midrashic anthology, possibly compiled by R. Simeon of Frankfurt, during the twelfth to thirteenth centuries in Europe.

20 For other modern adaptations and annotations, see Micha Joseph Bin Gorion, *Mimekor Yisrael: Classical Jewish Folktales*, abbr. and ann. edition, ed. Emanuel Bin Gorion, trans. Israel Meir Lask (Bloomington: Indiana University Press, 1990), no. 669 and no. 219, p. 427, respectively.

21 Louis Ginzberg, *The Legends of the Jews*, part 11, *Tohar* [Purity]*: The Book of Tales* (New York: Simon and Schuster, 1956), 95–106, 142–45.

22 Compare with the much later *ATU*, no. 555, "The Fisherman and His Wife."

23 A similar folktale appears in Jacob and Wilhelm Grimm, *The Original 1812 Grimm Fairytales*, trans. Oliver Loo (Morrisville, NC: Lulu Press, 2012), no. 19—which actually has the structure of a tragedy, rather than a comedy.

24 This angel does not appear in the Hebrew Bible but appears in the apocryphal Christian books of Enoch, is mentioned three times in the Talmud, and later in various kabbalistic works. For more on the kabbalistic approach to ethical education, see Patrick B. Koch, *Human Self-Perfection: A Re-Assessment of Kabbalistic Musar Literature of Sixteenth-Century Safed* (Los Angeles: Cherub Press, 2015); Koch, "Mysticism, Pietism, Morality: An Introduction," *European Journal of Jewish Studies* 14, no. 2 (2020): 169–76.

25 In fact, R. Ishmael b. Elisha (90–135 CE, a.k.a. *Ba'al ha-Baraita*) was a real Jewish sage and rabbinic scholar, who lived in the Land of Israel.

26 B. Talmud *Sanhedrin* 14a; *Avodah Zara* 8b, 17b, and 18b; and *Avot de-Rabbi Natan* 38. See also Ḥaim Naḥman Bialik and Yehoshua C. Ravnizky, *Sefer ha-Aggadah* (Tel Aviv: Dvir, 1948), no. 180; Judah David Eisenstein, ed., *Oṣar midrashim* (New York: Ktav, 1915), pt. 2, 439–50.

27 See also Archer Taylor, "The Biographical Pattern in Traditional Narrative," *Journal of the Folklore Institute* 1 (1964): 114–29; Alan Dundes, "The Hero Pattern and the Life of Jesus," in *Interpreting Folklore* (Bloomington: Indiana University Press, 1980), 223–62; Otto Rank, *The Myth of the Birth of the Hero and Other Writings* (New York: Vintage Books, 1964); Lord FitzRoy Raglan, *The Hero: A Study in Tradition, Myth and Drama* (New York: Vintage Books, 1956); Joseph Campbell, *The Hero with a Thousand Faces* (Princeton, NJ: Princeton University Press, 1949).

28 See Eisenstein, *Oṣar midrashim*.

29 B. Talmud *Ta'anit* 21a.

30 See Galit Brin, "Intercultural Aspects in 'Hibbur yafeh meha-Yeshuah': Genre, Thematics, and Editorial Trends." [In Hebrew.] PhD diss., Bar-Ilan University, 2017, 77–106

31 Nissim ben Jacob ibn Shahin, *An Elegant Composition Concerning Relief after Adversity*, trans. William M. Brinner (New Haven, CT: Yale University Press, 1977).

32 Edward J. Lowe, "For Want of a Nail," *Analysis* 40, no. 1 (1980): 50–52.

33 For Hebrew versions see *Menorat ha-Ma'or*, chap. 72, or M. J. Bin-Gorion, *Mi-Meqor Yisra'el*, no. 324; for English, see *Ma'aseh Book: Book of Jewish Tales and Legends*, trans. Moses Gaster (Philadelphia: Jewish Publication Society, 1981), vol. 2, 648.

34 For an understanding of the figure of the protagonist, see Aryeh Wineman, "*Ḥasid* and *Ḥakham*: Paradoxical Stories Found in Cabbalistic Ethical Literature," *Hebrew Studies* 25 (1984): 52–61; and his *Ethical Tales from the Kabbalah: Stories from the Kabbalistic Ethical Writings* (Philadelphia: Jewish Publication Society, 1999).

35 This is a well-known concept in Jewish mysticism: see Elliot R. Wolfson, "The Body in the Text: A Kabbalistic Theory of Embodiment," *Jewish Quarterly Review* 95, no. 3 (2005): 479–500.

36 For other modern adaptations and annotations, see Bin Gorion, *Mimekor Yisrael*, no. 324 and no. 102, 187, respectively.

37 Wolfson, "The Body in the Text," 479–500.

38 For example, see the long Jewish narrative tradition of Lilith in Saul Epstein and Sara Libby Robinson, "The Soul, Evil Spirits and the Undead: Vampires, Death and Burial in Jewish Folklore and Law," *Preternature: Critical and Historical Studies on the Preternatural* 1, no. 2 (2012): 232–51; Ruth Roded, "Jewish and Islamic Religious Feminist Exegesis of the Sacred Books: Adam, Woman and Gender," *Nashim: A Journal of Jewish Women's Studies and Gender Issues* 29 (2015): 56–80.

Chapter 4

1 For more on Jewish secularization, see Shmuel Feiner, *The Origins of Jewish Secularization in Eighteenth-Century Europe* [in Hebrew] (Jerusalem: Zalman Shazar Center, 2010).

2 As defined in this book's introduction, a "social exemplum" is a short anecdote meant to clarify a certain social convention. In the poetic theory of medieval literature, exempla are usually categorized as wisdom literature, along with parables, fables, and proverbs. However, the large corpus of *musar* tales supporting this study presents a slight shift from the classic usage of such tales, since their ultimate goal is, after all, to deal with universal problems rather than with intracultural Jewish law per se.

3 Yassif, *The Hebrew Folktale: History, Genre, Meaning* (Bloomington: Indiana University Press, 1994), 565n6.

4 Eli Yassif, "The Exemplary Story in *Sefer Ḥasidim*," *Tarbiṣ* (1988), 220–23.
5 This is based on Dan's definition. See Joseph Dan, "Categorization of the Narrative Material in Ashkenazi-Ḥasidic Literature," *Proceedings of the World Congress of Jewish Studies*, vol. 3, div. 3 (Jerusalem: World Union of Jewish Studies, 1969), 117.
6 Hans Robert Jauss, *Toward an Aesthetic of Reception*, trans. Timothy Bahti (Minneapolis: University of Minnesota Press, 1982), 3–45. Also see Robert C. Holub, *Reception Theory: A Critical Introduction* (London: Routledge, 1984), 53–81.
7 Pierre Bourdieu, *The Logic of Practice*, trans. Richard Nice (Stanford, CA: Stanford University Press, 1990), 52–65.
8 *ST* H310–H359 "Tests for Suitors." Again, in the *ATU*, one can find a category of tales, "Fidelity and Innocence" (ATU 880–99), which is part of a larger group of documented folktales on that theme from all over Europe.
9 See *ATU* 920–29 for "Clever Acts and Words" and Yassif, *Hebrew Folktale*, 627n125.
10 Note that, in the European folktale, the bride chooses the groom or, at least, she is present in the plot, whereas here the father of the bride chooses the groom, and the bride is absent. According to the Jewish tale, all the participants in the negotiation are men: the father, his friend, and the two candidates.
11 The William Davidson English edition of the b. Talmud is online at: www.sefaria.org.il/Sanhedrin.97a.7?lang=bi&with=all&lang2=en.
12 Note that this early tale ignores the well-known Jewish principle that the Sabbath may be desecrated to save human life. For a survey of the Jewish versions of this theme, see Amit Assis, "The Deposit of Trust," in *Encyclopedia of the Jewish Story: Sippur Okev Sippur*, ed. Yoav Elstein, and Avidov Lipsker, vol. 3 (Ramat-Gan: Bar-Ilan University Press, 2013), 83–114.

Chapter 5

1 Meyer H. Abrams, *A Glossary of Literary Terms*, 7th ed. (New York: Heinle & Heinle, 1999), 5–8. See also Simon Brittan, *Poetry, Symbol, and Allegory: Interpreting Metaphorical Language from Plato to the Present* (Charlottesville: University of Virginia Press, 2003).
2 The same problem occurs in other theological and philosophical areas dealing with the essence of divinity. For another example of the human attempt to explain the concept of the monotheistic God, see Ephraim E. Urbach, *The Sages: Their Concepts and Beliefs*, trans. Israel Abrahams (Jerusalem: Magnes Press, 1986), 15–28.
3 This has precedent in the Bible, where the phrase *Avir Ya'akov* (Gen. 49:24; Isa. 49:26; and Ps. 132:2, 5) was literally translated to visual illustrations

of knights in medieval Jewish manuscripts. See Sara Offenberg, "Jacob the Knight in Ezekiel's Chariot: Imagined Identity in Micrographic Decoration of an Ashkenazic Bible," *AJS* [Association for Jewish Studies] *Review* 40, no. 1 (2016): 1–16.

4 A historical Iranian unit for walking distance per hour, equal to about 6 kilometers per hour, so the distance indicated was about six thousand kilometers away.

5 There are a great number of essays and explanations regarding this theme, wherein the same biographical pattern is shared by many cultural heroes: see Joseph Campbell, *The Hero with a Thousand Faces* (Princeton, NJ: Princeton University Press, 1968); Evans Smith, *The Hero in Literature: Parables of Poesis* (Lanham, MD: University Press of America, 1997); and Dean A. Miller, *The Epic Hero* (Baltimore, MD: Johns Hopkins University Press, 2000).

6 For more on the connection between faith and text, see David Lawton, *Faith, Text, and History* (Charlottesville: University of Virginia Press, 1990).

7 See David Stern, "Rhetoric and *Midrash*: The Case of the *Mashal*," *Prooftexts* 1, no. 3 (1981): 261–91; Isaac B. Gottlieb, "*Mashal le-Melekh*: The Search for Solomon," *Hebrew Studies* 51 (2010): 107–21.

8 See *ATU* 577 "The King's Tasks." See also *ST* motifs: H335 "Tasks Assigned Suitors, Bride as Prize," and H1242 "Youngest Brother Alone Succeeds on Quest."

9 See *ATU* 554 "The Grateful Animals."

10 See *ATU* 550A "God and the Three Brothers" and *ATU* 160 "Grateful Animals and Ungrateful Man."

11 Viktor Shklovsky, "Sterne's *Tristram Shandy*: Stylistic Commentary," in *Russian Formalist Criticism: Four Essays*, 2nd ed., trans. Lee T. Lemon and Marion J. Reis (Lincoln: University of Nebraska Press, 2012), 25–57. For a classic approach to folktales, see Vladimir Propp, *Morphology of the Folktale*, trans. Laurence Scott (Austin: University of Texas Press, 1968).

12 See, for example, the recent issue of the *European Journal of Jewish Studies*, which was devoted entirely to *musar* essays. In his introduction, the editor notes that there is no clear definition of *musar* literature. Patrick B. Koch, "Mysticism, Pietism, Morality: An Introduction," *European Journal of Jewish Studies* 14, no. 2 (2020): 169–76. Also see the words of Ilaria Briata in the same issue: "*Musar* itself can hardly be described as a literary genre, as this technical label does not recount the heterogeneity of the content and form of Jewish moralistic texts": "Repentance through Fear: Cosmic and Body Horror in Shēveṭ Musar," 264–84.

Conclusions and Final Remarks

1 David Finkelstein, *An Introduction to Book History* (New York: Routledge, 2005). Craig Kallendorf, *The Virgillian Tradition: Book History and the History of Reading in Early Modern Europe* (Aldershot, UK: Ashgate-Variorum, 2007); Guglielmo Cavallo and Roger Chartier, eds., *A History of Reading in the West*, trans. L. G. Cochrane (Amherst: University of Massachusetts Press, 1999); Chartier, *The Order of Books* (Stanford, CA: Stanford University Press, 1994); Alberto Manguel, *A History of Reading* (New York: Penguin, 1996).

2 Albert Thibaudet, *French Literature from 1789 to Our Era*, trans. Charles Lam Markmann (New York: Funk & Wagnalls, 1967).

3 Pierre Bourdieu, *Distinction: A Social Critique of the Judgement of Taste*, trans. Richard Nice (Stanford, CA: Stanford University Press, 1984); Bourdieu, *The Field of Cultural Production* (Cambridge, UK: Polity Press 1993), 112–20.

4 Rubin, "*Sefer Lev Ṭov* (Prague, 1620): The First Edition of the Book?" *Zuṭot: Perspectives on Jewish Culture* 5, no. 1 (2008): 121–27; Rubin, and Zelda Kahan Newman, "Pious Wrappings, Troubling Insides: Four Different Genres of Ashkenazic Literature," *Journal of Modern Jewish Studies* 7, no. 3 (2008): 269–82.

5 Vered Tohar, *The Book of Tales, Sermons and Legends (Ferrara 1554): An Anthology of Hebrew Stories from the Print Era* (Tel Aviv: Hakibbutz Hameuchad, 2016); Tohar, "Distribution of Narrative Traditions in Europe and the Middle East: The Products of the Usque Printing House," *Aliento* 9, ed. Marie-Sol Ortola: 175–94; Tohar, "Does Print Matter? The 16th Century Printed Editions of the Hebrew Essay '*Midrash 'Aseret ha-Dibrot*'," *Aliento* 10 (2018): 413–26.

6 Tohar, "The Exegesis of Baḥya ben Asher for Gen. 15:7," *European Journal of Jewish Studies* 9 (2015): 132–51.

7 Isaiah Tishby and Joseph Dan, comps., *Mivḥar Sifrut ha-Musar: Praqim Nivḥarim be-Ṣēruf Ṣiyunim, Be'urim ve-Mevo'ot* [Selected *musar* literature] (Tel Aviv: M. Newman, 1970), ix. See also Stanley Cavell, *Cities of Words: Pedagogical Letters on a Register of the Moral Life* (Cambridge, MA: Harvard University Press, 2004), 54–60.

8 Elbaum, *Openness and Insularity: Late Sixteenth Century Jewish Literature in Poland and Ashkenaz* [in Hebrew] (Jerusalem: Magnes Press, 1990), 223–42.

9 This could be reinforced by the work of Warren Z. Harvey, "Ethical Theories among Medieval Jewish Philosophers," in *The Oxford Handbook of Jewish Ethics and Morality*, ed. Elliot N. Dorff and Jonathan K. Crane (Oxford: Oxford University Press, 2013), 84–101.

10 Avriel Bar-Levav, "Magic in Jewish Ethical Literature," [in Hebrew], *Tarbiṣ* 72, no. 3 (2003): 389–414.

11 Simon J. Bronner, "Practice Theory in Folklore and Folklife Studies," *Folklore* 123 (2012): 23–47.

12 See also an important analysis by Ulrich Marzolf, "What Is Folklore Good for? On Dealing with Undesirable Cultural Expression," *Journal of Folklore Research* 35, no. 1 (1998): 5–16.

13 For more on the classification of folktale types, see Hans Georg Uther, *The Types of International Folktales: A Classification and Bibliography* (Helsinki: Suomalainen Tiedeakatemia, 2004).

Appendix 1

1 The sources of this bibliographical information are Isaak A. Benjacob's, *Ozar ha-sepharim: Thesaurus librorum hebraicorum tam impressorum quam manu scriptorium* [The Treasure of books, in Hebrew], ed. Jacob Benjacob (Vilna: Romm Press, 1880); Ḥaim Dov Friedberg, *Bēt Eqed Sfarim: Leksiqon Bibliografi* (Tel Aviv: Bar-Yoda, 1956); and also see Yeshayahu Vinograd, *Thesaurus of the Hebrew Book* (Jerusalem: Institute for Digital Bibliography, 1994).

2 The name of this work refers to the palm tree underneath which Deborah the Prophetess, wife of Lappidoth, would sit and give consultations to Israelites who needed help making difficult decisions: Judges 4:5.

3 For a recent, annotated Hebrew translation of Baḥya ibn Paquda, see Binyamin Abrahamov, *Book of Direction to the Duties of the Heart* [in Hebrew] (Ramat-Gan: Bar-Ilan University Press, 2019). For more on the translation, see Barak Avirbach, "Rabbinic Entries in R. Judah ibn Tibbon's Translation of *Duties of the Hearts*," in *Studies in Rabbinic Hebrew*, ed. Shai Heijmans (Cambridge: Cambridge University Press, 2020), 119–53.

4 See Abrahamov, *Bahya Ibn Paquda*, and his "The Sources of Rabenu Baḥya ibn Pakuda [Paquda] in *Ḥovot ha-Levavot*" [in Hebrew], *Oreshet* 9 (2020): 7–38.

5 See also Stephen Samuel Wise, *The Improvement of the Moral Qualities: An Ethical Treatise of the Eleventh Century by Solomon Ibn Gabirol* (New York: Columbia University Press, 1901).

6 Wise, *Improvement of the Moral Qualities*, 41, and online, accessed Feb. 7, 2022, archive.org/stream/cu31924014141968/cu31924014141968_djvu.txt.

7 Sarah Kats, "The Author of *Mivḥar ha-Peninim*" [in Hebrew], *Sinai* 103 (1989): 169–72.

8 See Yehuda Razhabi, "The Muslim Sources of *Mivḥar ha-Peninim*" [in Hebrew], *Sinai* 102 (1988): 93–102; Noaḥ Braun, "Studies in *Mivḥar ha-Peninim*" [in Hebrew], *Tarbiṣ* 19 (1948): 45–52.

9 Haim Hillel Ben-Sasson, "Punishment, Sin and Repentance: The Uniqueness of *Sha'arē Teshuvah*" [in Hebrew], *Tarbiṣ* 71 (2019): 63–106.

10 Gavriel Itzhak Ravena, "*Ma'alot ha-Middot*: Its Nature and Characteristics," in *A Wise-Hearted Woman: In Memoriam of Dr. Sara Fraenkel*, ed. Bracha Yaniv (Jerusalem: Art Plus, 2011), 25–52.

11 Ravena, "*Ma'alot ha-Middot*."

12 For more on *Menorat ha-Ma'or*, see Israel M. Ta-Shma, "The Riddle of the Book *Menorat ha-Ma'or* and Its Solution" [in Hebrew], *Tarbiṣ* 64, no. 3 (1995): 395–400.

13 Yoel Marciano, "The Rise of Non-Religious Literature in Late Medieval Spain and Its Reflection in *Menorat ha-Ma'or* of R. Isaac Aboab," *Sefarad* 79, no. 2 (2020): 411–45.

14 See the first printed edition (Constantinople: Astruc of Toulon, 1513), 1.

15 For more on the origins of *Orḥot Ṣaddiqim*, see Jeffrey Woolf, "When Was the Book *Orḥot Ṣaddiqim* written?" [in Hebrew], *Qiryat Sefer* 64, no. 1 (1993), 321–22.

16 Assaf Navarro, "Editing and Theology of Orḥot Zaddiqim" [in Hebrew], MA thesis, Hebrew University of Jerusalem, 2002.

17 Avriel Bar-Levav, "When I Was Alive: Jewish Ethical Wills as Egodocuments" [in Hebrew], in *Egodocuments and History: Autobiographical Writing in Its Social Context since the Middle Ages*, ed. Rudolf Dekker (Hilversum, Neth.: Uitgeverij Verloren, 2002), 47–59.

18 In regard to the bilingual situation of Jewish culture and eighteenth-century *musar* literature, see Jan Baumgarten, "Between Translation and Commentary: The Bilingual Editions of the '*Kav Hayosher*' by Tsvi Hirsh Koidanover," *Journal of Modern Jewish Studies* 3, no. 3 (2004), 269–78; Baumgarten, *Introduction to Old Yiddish Literature* (Oxford: Oxford University Press, 2005); and Baumgarten, "Eighteenth-Century Ethico-Mysticism in Central Europe," *Studia Rosenthaliana* 41 (2009), 29–51.

19 R. Zvi Hirsch Kaidanover, *Qav ha-yashar* (Frankfurt am Main, 1706), 1.

20 Kaidanover, *Qav ha-yashar*, 1.

21 See *Shēveṭ Musar* (Constantinople, 1712), 1.

Bibliography

Aarne, Antti. *The Types of the Folktale*. Trans. S. Thompson. Helsinki: Soumalainen Tiedeakatemia, 1961.

Abarbanel, Nitza. *Havah ve-Lilith* [Eve and Lilith]. [In Hebrew.] Ramat-Gan: Bar-Ilan University Press, 1994.

Abrahamov, Binyamin. *Bahya Ibn Paquda: The Book of Direction to the Duties of the Heart*. [In Hebrew.] Ramat-Gan: Bar-Ilan University Press, 2019.

———. "The Sources of Rabenu Baḥya ibn Pakuda [Paquda] in *Hovot Hal-evavot*." [In Hebrew.] *Oreshet* 9 (2020): 7–38.

Abrams, Meyer H. *A Glossary of Literary Terms*. 7th ed. New York: Heinle & Heinle, 1999.

Abramson Shraga, comp. *R. Nissim Ga'on: Ḥamishah sfarim: Sridim mey-hibburav yots'im la-or 'al pi kitvey yad* [Rabbi Nissim Gaon: Five Books: Remnants of Essays Published as Manuscripts]. [In Hebrew.] Jerusalem: Mekitse Nirdamim, 1965.

Alberghini Jennifer. "Knowing Nature: Bear-Human Bestiality in the *Gesta Romanorum*." *Folklore* 132(2) (2021): 189–207.

Assis, Amit. "The Deposit of Trust." [In Hebrew.] In *Encyclopedia of the Jewish Story: Sippur Okev Sippur*, edited by Yoav Elstein, and Avidov Lipsker, vol. 3, 83–114. Ramat-Gan: Bar-Ilan University Press, 2013.

Bailey, Harold Walter. "'Bisclavret' in Marie de France." *Cambridge Medieval Celtic Studies* 1 (1981): 95–97.

Bakhtin, Mikhail. *Problems of Dostoevsky's Poetics*. Edited by Caryl Emerson. Minneapolis: University of Minnesota Press, 1984.

———. *Speech Genres and Other Late Essays*. Translated by V. W. McGee. Austin: Texas University Press, 1986.

Bar-Itzhak, Haya, and Idit Pintel-Ginsberg, eds. *The Power of the Tale: The Jubilee Book of IFA, Israel Folklore Archive*. [In Hebrew.] Haifa: Haifa University Press, 2008.

Bar-Levav, Avriel. "Magic in Jewish Ethical Literature." [In Hebrew.] *Tarbiṣ* 72, no. 3 (2003): 389–414.

———. "When I Was Alive: Jewish Ethical Wills as Egodocuments." [In Hebrew.] In *Egodocuments and History: Autobiographical Writing in Its Social Context since the Middle Ages*, edited by R. Dekker, 47–59. Hilversum, Neth.: Uitgeverij Verloren, 2002.

Baumgarten, Jan. "Between Translation and Commentary: The Bilingual Editions of the '*Kav Hayosher*' by Tsvi Hirsh Koidanover." *Journal of Modern Jewish Studies* 3, no. 3 (2004): 269–78.

———. "Eighteenth-Century Ethico-Mysticism in Central Europe." *Studia Rosenthaliana* 41 (2009): 29–51.

———. *Introduction to Old Yiddish Literature*. Oxford: Oxford University Press, 2005.

Beit-Arie, Malachi. "The Relationship between Early Hebrew Printing and Handwritten Books: Attachment or Detachment?" [In Hebrew.] *Scripta Hierosolymitana* 29 (1989): 1–26.

Belsey, Catherine. "Problems of Literary Theory: The Problem of Meaning." *New Literary History* 14, no. 1 (1982): 175–82.

Ben-Amos, Dan. "'Context' in Context," *Western Folklore* 52, 2/4 (1993), 209–26.

———, ed. *Folklore Genres*. Austin: University of Texas Press, 1976.

———. *Ha-sifrut ha-'amamit ha-Yehudit* [Jewish folk literature]. [In Hebrew.] Jerusalem: Magnes, 2006.

———. "Jewish Folk Literature." *Oral Tradition* 14, no. 1 (1999): 140–274.

———. "Jewish Studies and Jewish Folklore." *Proceedings of the World Congress of Jewish Studies, Division D* (1989): 1–20.

Benjacob, Isaak A., comp. Ozar ha-Sepharim: Thesaurus librorum Hebraicorum tam impressorum quam manu scriptorium [The treasure of books. In Hebrew]. Edited by Jacob Benjacob. New York: Jerusalem Publishing, 1880.

Berthoff, Warner. *Literature and the Continuances of Virtue*. Princeton, NJ: Princeton University Press, 2014.

Bialik, Ḥaim Naḥman, and Yehoshua C. Ravnizky, eds. *Sefer ha-Aggadah*. [In Hebrew.] Tel Aviv: Dvir, 1948.

Bibring, Tovi. "In *Ictu Oculi*: Reflections on Wolf and Beast by Berechia ha-Naqdan in the Context of Its Contemporary Versions." *Comparative Literature Studies* 56, no. 2 (2019): 374–401.

Bin Gorion [Berdichevsky], Micha Joseph, comp. *Mimekor Yisrael: Classical Jewish Folktales*. Abbr. and ann. ed. Edited by Emanuel Bin Gorion. Translated by Israel Meir Lask. Annotated by Dan Ben-Amos. Bloomington: Indiana University Press, 1990.

———. *Mi-Meqor Yisra'el.* [In Hebrew.] Tel Aviv: Dvir, 1938.

Bor, Harris. "Enlightenment Values, Jewish Ethics: The *Haskalah*'s Transformation of the Traditional *Musar* Genre." In *New Perspectives on Haskalah*, edited by Shmuel Feiner and Dov Sorkin, 48–63. London: Littman Library of Jewish Civilization, 2001.

Bourdieu, Pierre. *Distinction: A Social Critique of the Judgement of Taste*. Translated by Richard Nice. Stanford, CA: Stanford University Press, 1984.

———. *The Field of Cultural Production*. Cambridge, UK: Polity Press, 1993.

———. *The Logic of Practice*. Translated by Richard Nice. Stanford, CA: Stanford University Press, 1990.

———. *Outline of a Theory of Practice*. Translated by Richard Nice. Cambridge: Cambridge University Press, 1977.

Briata, Ilaria. "Repentance through Fear: Cosmic and Body Horror in *Shēveṭ Musar.*" *European Journal of Jewish Studies* 14, no. 2 (2020): 264–84.

Brin Galit. "Intercultural Aspects in 'Hibbur yafeh meha-Yeshuah': Genre, Thematics, and Editorial Trends." [In Hebrew.] PhD diss., Bar-Ilan University, 2017.

Brittan, Simon. *Poetry, Symbol, and Allegory: Interpreting Metaphorical Language from Plato to the Present*. Charlottesville: University of Virginia Press, 2003.

Bronner, Simon J. "Folk Logic: Interpretation and Explanation in Folkloristics." *Western Folklore* 65, no. 4 (2006): 401–33.

———. "Practice Theory in Folklore and Folklife Studies." *Folklore* 123 (2012): 23–47.

Bruckner, Matilda Tomaryn. "Of Men and Beasts in 'Bisclavret'." *Romanic Review* 82 (1991): 251–69.

Bruner, Jerome S. *Relevance of Education*. New York: Norton Library, 1973.

Campbell, Joseph. *The Hero with a Thousand Faces* Princeton, NJ: Princeton University Press, 1949.

Cavallo, Guglielmo, and Roger Chartier, eds. *A History of Reading in the West*. Translated by L. G. Cochrane. Amherst: University of Massachusetts Press, 1999.

Cavell, Stanley. *Cities of Words: Pedagogical Letters on a Register of the Moral Life*. Cambridge, MA: Harvard University Press, 2004.

Chartier, Roger. *The Order of Books*. Stanford, CA: Stanford University Press, 1994.

Childs, Peter, and Roger Fowler, eds. *The Routledge Dictionary of Literary Terms*. London: Routledge, 2006.

Classen Albrecht. "Alcohol, Drunkenness, and Excess: Consumption and Transgression in European Medieval and Early Modern Literature." *Neophilologus:*

An International Journal of Modern and Medieval Language and Literature 126 (2022): 1–22.

———. "From the *Gesta Romanorum* to Werner Bergengruen: Literary Mirrors for Princes from the Late Middle Ages to the Twentieth Century." *Amsterdamer Beiträge zur Älteren Germanistik* 81, no. 1 (2021): 98–123.

Colahan Clark. "Episodes in Persiles and Sigismunda Shaped by 'Byzantine Tales' from the *Gesta Romanorum*." *Hipogrifo* 3, no. 1 (2015): 129–39.

Collins, Terry. "Intimations of Feminism in Ancient Athens: Euripides' Medea." *Sydney Studies in English* 26 (2000): 3–24.

Cornford, Francis Macdonald. *The Origin of Attic Comedy*. London: Edward Arnold, 1914.

Corrigan, Robert. *Comedy: Meaning and Form*. New York: Harper & Row, 1965.

Cuddon, John A. *A Dictionary of Literary Terms and Literary Theory*. 5th ed. Chichester: Wiley, 2013.

Dan, Joseph. "Categorization of the Narrative Material in Ashkenazi-Ḥasidic Literature." [In Hebrew.] *Proceedings of the World Congress of Jewish Studies* 3, no. 3 (1969): 117.

———. "Ethical Literature." In *Encyclopaedia Judaica*, 2nd ed., edited by Michael Berenbaum and Fred Skolnik, vol. 6, 525–31. Detroit: Macmillan Reference 2007.

———. *Hebrew Ethical and Homiletical Literature*. [In Hebrew.] Jerusalem: Keter, 1975.

———. *The Hebrew Story in the Middle Ages: Studies of Its History*. [In Hebrew.] Jerusalem: Keter, 1974.

———. On Sanctity: Religion, Ethics and Mysticism in Judaism and Other Religions. [In Hebrew.] Jerusalem: Magnes Press, 1998.

Darnton, Robert. *The Great Cat Massacre and Other Episodes in French Cultural History*. New York: Basic Books, 1984.

Davenport, Tony. *Medieval Narrative*. Oxford: Oxford University Press, 2004.

Dundes, Alan. "From Etic to Emic Units in the Structural Study of Folktales." *Journal of American Folklore* 75 (1962): 95–105.

———. "The Hero Pattern and the Life of Jesus." In *Interpreting Folklore*, 223–62. Bloomington: Indiana University Press, 1980.

———, ed. *The Study of Folklore*. Englewood Cliffs, NJ: Prentice-Hall, 1964.

Eberhard Hermes, ed. *The Disciplina Clericalis of Petrus Alfonsi*. Berkeley: University of California Press, 1977.

Eisenstein, Elizabeth L. *The Printing Press as an Agent of Change: Communication and Cultural Transformations in Early-Modern Europe*. Cambridge: Cambridge University Press, 1979.

Eisenstein, Judah David. *Oṣar midrashim*. Pt. 2. [In Hebrew.] New York: Ktav, 1915.

Elbaum, Jacob. *Openness and Insularity: Late Sixteenth Century Jewish Literature in Poland and Ashkenaz.* [In Hebrew.] Jerusalem: Magnes Press, 1990.

Epstein, Saul, and Sara Libby Robinson. "The Soul, Evil Spirits and the Undead: Vampires, Death and Burial in Jewish Folklore and Law." *Preternature: Critical and Historical Studies on the Preternatural* 1, no. 2 (2012): 232–51.

Feiner, Shmuel. *The Origins of Jewish Secularization in Eighteenth-Century Europe.* [In Hebrew.] (Jerusalem: Zalman Shazar Center, 2010).

Feliks, Judah. "Dog." In *Encyclopaedia Judaica*, 2nd ed., edited by Michael Berenbaum and Fred Skolnik, vol. 5, 733. Jerusalem: Macmillan Reference, 2007.

Finkelstein, David. *An Introduction to Book History.* New York: Routledge, 2005.

Fitzgerald, Robert. *Homer: The Odyssey.* New York: Vintage Books, 1990.

Fludernik, Monika. *An Introduction to Narratology.* Translated by Patricia Hausler and Monika Fludernik. London: Routledge, 2006.

Ford, Gabriel. "Framing, Parataxis and the Poetics of Exemplarity in Petrus Alfonsi's *Disciplina Clericalis.*" *Medieval Encounters* 21, no. 1 (2015): 26–49.

———. "Sociality at the Margins of Petrus Alfonsi's *Disciplina Clericalis.*" *Digital Philology: A Journal of Medieval Cultures* 9, no. 1 (2020): 27–46.

Friedberg, Ḥaim Dov. *Bēt Eqed Sfarim: Leksiqon Bibliografi.* [In Hebrew.] Tel Aviv: Bar-Yoda, 1956.

Friedrich, Udo. "Zur Verdinglichtung der Werte den *Gesta Romanorum.*" In *Dingkulturen: Objekte in Literatur, Kunst und Gesellschaft der Vormoderne*, edited by Anna Mühlerr, Heike Sahn, Monika Schausten, and Bruno Quast, 249–66. Berlin: Walter de Gruyter, 2016.

Garb, Jonathan. "From Fear to Awe in Luzzatto's *Mesillat Yesharim.*" *European Journal of Jewish Studies* 14, no. 2 (2020): 285–99.

Gaster, Moses. *The Exempla of the Rabbis.* New York: Ktav, 1968.

———, trans. *Ha-Levi, Elazar ben Asher: The Chronicles of Jerahmeel.* New York: Ktav, 1971.

———, trans. *Ma'aseh Book.* Philadelphia: Jewish Publication Society, 1981.

Ginzberg, Louis. *The Legends of the Jews.* New York: Simon and Schuster, 1956.

Gottlieb, Isaac B. "*Mashal le-Melekh*: The Search for Solomon." *Hebrew Studies* 51 (2010): 107–21.

Gries, Zeev. *The Book as an Agent of Culture, 1700–1900.* [In Hebrew.] Tel Aviv: Hakibbutz Hameuchad, 2002.

———. *The Book in the Jewish World, 1700–1900.* Rev. ed. Oxford: Littman Library of Jewish Civilization, 2010.

———. *Conduct Literature (Regimen Vitae): Its History and Place in the Life of Beshṭian Ḥasidism.* [In Hebrew.] Jerusalem: Bialik Institute, 1989.

———. *The Hebrew Book: An Outline of Its History.* [In Hebrew.] Jerusalem: Bialik Institute, 2015.

Harris, Marvin. "History and Significance of the Emic/Etic Distinction." *Annual Review of Anthropology* 5 (1976): 329–50.

Harrison, Jane. *Themis: A Study of Social Origins of Greek Religion.* Cambridge: Cambridge University Press, 1912.

Hasan-Rokem, Galit. *Tales of a Neighbourhood: Jewish Narrative Dialogue in Late Antiquity.* Berkeley: University of California Press, 2003.

Hendler, Hana. "Nachum of Gamzu and His Errand to King Caesar." [In Hebrew.] In *Encyclopedia of the Jewish Story: Sippur Okev Sippur*, vol. 1, 247–60, edited by Yoav Elstein, Avidov Lipsker, and Rella Kushelevsky. Ramat-Gan: Bar-Ilan University Press, 2004.

Hess, Cordelia. Social Imagery in Middle Low German: Didactic Literature and Metaphorical Representation (1470–1517). (Leiden: Brill, 2013).

Hirschberg, Haim Ze'ev. *Ḥibbur Yafeh meha-Yeshu'ah.* [In Hebrew.] Jerusalem: Rav Kook Talmudical Research Institute, 1954.

Hokenson, Jan. *The Idea of Comedy: History, Theory, Critique.* Madison, NJ: Fairleigh Dickinson University Press, 2006.

Holub, Robert C. *Reception Theory: A Critical Introduction.* London: Routledge, 1984.

Houston, Robert A. *Literacy in Early Modern Europe: Culture and Education, 1500–1800.* London: Longman, 1988.

Hursthouse, Rosalind. *On Virtue Ethics.* Oxford: Oxford University Press, 2010.

Idel, Moshe. "On Rabbi Zvi Hirsh Koidanover's *Sefer Qav ha-Yashar.*" [In German.] In *Judische Kultur in Frankfurt am Main von den Anfängen bis zur Gegenwart*, edited by Karl E. Grözinger, 123–33. Wiesbaden, Ger.: Harrassowitz, 1997.

Iser, Wolfgang, *The Act of Reading: A Theory of Aesthetic Response.* Baltimore: Johns Hopkins University Press, 1978.

———. "The Reading Process: A Phenomenological Approach." *New Literary History* 3, no. 2 (1972): 279–99.

Jauss, Hans R. *Toward an Aesthetic of Reception.* Translated by Timothy Bahti. Minneapolis: University of Minnesota Press, 1989.

Kallendorf, Craig. *The Virgillian Tradition: Book History and the History of Reading in Early Modern Europe.* Aldershot, UK: Ashgate-Variorum, 2007.

Katzenellenbogen, Adolf. *Allegories of the Virtues and Vices in Medieval Art: From Early Christian Times to the Thirteenth Century.* Translated by Alan J. Crick. New York: Norton Library, 1964.

Koch, Patrick B. *Human Self-Perfection: A Re-Assessment of Kabbalistic Musar Literature of Sixteenth-Century Safed.* Los Angeles: Cherub Press, 2015.

———. "Mysticism, Pietism, Morality: An Introduction," *European Journal of Jewish Studies* 14, no. 2 (2020): 169–76.

Kushelevsky, Rella, "*Midrash 'Aseret ha-Dibrot'* in MS Parma 2269." [In Hebrew.] *Jerusalem Studies in Jewish Folklore* 29 (2015): 33–77.

———. *Penalty and Temptation: Hebrew Tales in Ashkenaz, MS Parma 2295 (de-Rossi 563).* [In Hebrew.] Jerusalem, Magnes: 2010.

———. *Tales in Context: Sefer ha-Ma'asim in Medieval Northern France.* Detroit: Wayne State University Press, 2017.

Lawton, David. *Faith, Text, and History.* Charlottesville: University of Virginia Press, 1990.

Leach, Maria, ed. *Standard Dictionary of Folklore, Mythology and Legend.* New York: Funk & Wagnalls, 1949.

Leslie, Andrew. "How Stories Argue: The Deep Roots of Storytelling in Political Rhetoric." *Storytelling, Self, Society* 11, no. 1 (2015): 66–84.

Levin, Harry. *Playboys and Killjoys: An Essay on the Theory and Practice of Comedy.* New York: Oxford University Press, 1987.

Lipsker, Avidov. "Matya ben Ḥeresh." [In Hebrew.] In *Encyclopedia of the Jewish Story: Sippur Okev Sippur,* vol. 2, edited by Yoav Elstein, Avidov Lipsker, and Rella Kushelevsky, 275–90. Ramat-Gan: Bar-Ilan University, 2009.

Lowe, Edward J. "For Want of a Nail." *Analysis* 40, no. 1 (1980): 50–52.

Manguel, Alberto. *A History of Reading.* New York: Penguin, 1996.

Marzolph, Ulrich. "What Is Folklore Good for? On Dealing with Undesirable Cultural Expression." *Journal of Folklore Research* 35, no. 1 (1998): 5–16.

McKitterick, Rosamond, ed. *The Uses of Literacy in Early Mediaeval Europe.* Cambridge: Cambridge University Press, 1992.

Merchant, William Moelwyn. *Comedy: The Critical Idiom.* London: Methuen, 1972.

Miller, Dean A. *The Epic Hero.* Baltimore, MD: Johns Hopkins University Press, 2000.

Murray, Gilbert. "Excurses on the Ritual Forms Preserved in Greek Tragedy." In *Themis: A Study of Social Origins of Greek Religion*, edited by Jane Harrison, 341–63. Cambridge: Cambridge University Press, 1912.

Navarro, Assaf. "Editing and Theology of Orhot Zaddiqim." [In Hebrew.] MA thesis, Hebrew University of Jerusalem, 2002.

Neumann, Erich. *The Great Mother: An Analysis of the Archetype.* 2nd ed. Translated by Ralph Manheim. Princeton, NJ: Princeton University Press, 1974.

Neusner, Jacob. "Bestiary, Rabbinic." In *Encyclopaedia of Judaism*, Brill Online Reference Works, accessed Feb. 10, 2022. https://referenceworks.brillonline.com/entries/encyclopaedia-of-judaism/bestiary-rabbinic-COM_0017?s.num=0.

Newhauser, Richard. *The Treatise on Vices and Virtues in Latin and the Vernacular.* Turnhout, Belg.: Brepols, 1993.

Nissim b. Jacob ibn Shāhīn. *An Elegant Composition Concerning Relief after Adversity: An Eleventh-Century Book of Comfort.* Translated by William M. Brinner. New Haven, CT: Yale University Press, 1977.

Obermann, Julian, ed. *The Arabic Original of Ibn Shâhîn's Book of Comfort Known as the Ḥibbûr Yaphê of R. Nissîm b. Ya'aqobh.* [In Arabic, Hebrew, English.] New Haven, CT: Yale University Press, 1933.

Offenberg, Sara. "Jacob the Knight in Ezekiel's Chariot: Imagined Identity in Micrographic Decoration of an Ashkenazic Bible." *AJS* [Association for Jewish Studies] *Review* 40, no. 1 (2016): 1–16.

Ong, Walter J. *Orality and Literacy: The Technologizing of the World.* New York: Routledge, 2012.

Palmer, David J., ed. *Comedy: Developments in Criticism.* Basingstoke, UK: Macmillan, 1984.

Perry, Micha. *Tradition and Transformation: Knowledge Transmission among European Jews in the Middle Ages.* [In Hebrew.] Tel Aviv: Hakibbutz Hameuchad, 2010.

Preuss, Julius. *Biblical and Talmudic Medicine.* Translated and edited by Fred Rosner. Northvale, NJ: Jason Aronson, 1993.

Propp, Vladimir. *Morphology of the Folktale.* Translated by Laurence Scott. Austin: University of Texas Press, 1968.

Quinn, Edward. *A Dictionary of Literary and Thematic Terms.* 2nd ed. New York: Facts on File, 2006.

Raglan, Lord FitzRoy. *The Hero: A Study in Tradition, Myth and Drama.* New York: Vintage Books, 1956.

Rank, Otto. *The Myth of the Birth of the Hero and Other Writings.* New York: Vintage Books, 1964.

Refael-Vivante, Revital. "Charity as a Value and Norm in *Mishlei Shu'alim* by Rabbi Berechia ha-Naqdan." In *Berechia ben Natronai ha-Naqdan's Works and Their Reception*, edited by Tamás Visi, Tovi Bibring, and Daniel Soukop, 53–74. Turnhout, Belg.: Brepols, 2019.

———. "Of Lions and Foxes: Power and Rule in Hebrew Medieval Fables." *Revista de Paz y Conflictos* 2 (2009): 24–43.

Rimmon-Kenan, Shlomith. *Narrative Fiction: Contemporary Poetics.* London: Methuen, 1983.

Roded, Ruth. "Jewish and Islamic Religious Feminist Exegesis of the Sacred Books: Adam, Woman and Gender." *Nashim: A Journal of Jewish Women's Studies and Gender Issues* 29 (2015): 56–80.

Rotman, David. *Dragons, Demons and Wonderous Realms: The Marvelous in Medieval Hebrew Narrative*. [In Hebrew.] Be'er-Sheva: Kinneret, Zmora-Bitan, Dvir Publishing & Heksherim Institute, 2016.

Rotunda, Dominic Peter. *Motif Index of the Italian Novella in Prose*. Bloomington: Indiana University Press, 1942.

Rozik, Eli. *The Roots of Theatre: Rethinking Ritual and Other Theories of Origin*. Iowa City: University of Iowa Press, 2002.

Rubin, Noga. *Conqueror of Hearts: Sefer Lev Ṭov by R. Isaac Ben Eliakim of Posen (Prague, 1620): A Central Ethical Book in Yiddish*. [In Hebrew.] Tel Aviv: Hakibbutz Hameuchad, 2013.

———. "*Sefer Lev Ṭov* (Prague, 1620): The First Edition of the Book?" *Zuṭot: Perspectives on Jewish Culture* 5, no. 1 (2008): 121–27.

Rubin, Noga, and Zelda Kahan Newman. "Pious Wrappings, Troubling Insides: Four Different Genres of Ashkenazic Literature." *Journal of Modern Jewish Studies* 7, no. 3 (2008): 269–82.

Sanjuan, Oscar Abenojar. "On the Sources of the Exemplum XXIII of the *Disciplina Clericalis* and Its Survival in the Iberian and Latin American Traditions." *Hispanofilia* 193 (2021): 165–79.

Sartre, Jean-Paul. "The Look." In *Being and Nothingness: A Phenomenological Essay on Ontology*, translated by Hazel E. Barnes, 340–400. New York: Washington Square Press, 1992.

Schwartz, Elias. "The Problem of Literary Genres." *Criticism* 13, no. 2 (1971): 113–30.

Schwarzbaum, Haim. *International Folklore Motifs in Petrus Alfonsi's "Disciplina Clericalis."* Madrid: Talleres Graficos, 1961–63.

———. *The Mishlē Shu'alim (Fox Fables) of Rabbi Berechiah ha-Nakdan: A Study in Comparative Folklore and Fable Lore*. Kiron, Isr.: Institute for Jewish and Arab Folklore Research, 1979.

Segal, Erich. *The Death of Comedy*. Cambridge, MA: Harvard University Press, 2001.

Shaanan, Avraham, ed. *Dictionary of Modern Literature*. [In Hebrew.] Tel Aviv: Yavne Publishing House, 1978.

Shapira, Anat. *Midrash 'Aseret ha-Dibrot' (A Midrash on the Ten Commandments): Text, Sources and Interpretation*. [In Hebrew.] Jerusalem: Bialik Institute, 2005.

Shenhar, Aliza. *From a Folktale to a Children's Tale*. [In Hebrew.] Haifa: University of Haifa Press, 1982.

Shmeruk, Chone. *Chapters in Yiddish Literature*. [In Hebrew.] Tel Aviv: Tel Aviv University Press, 1978.

———. *Yiddish Literature in Poland.* [In Hebrew.] Jerusalem: Magnes Press, 1981.

Shoshany, Ronit. "A Study of Two Legends in *Midrash Ruth Zuṭa* in Light of *Ḥibbur Yafeh meha-Yeshu'ah.*" [In Hebrew.] *Jewish Studies: The Internet Journal* 7 (2008): 81–103.

Singer, Peter. *Applied Ethics.* Oxford: Oxford University Press, 1986.

Smith, Evans. *The Hero in Literature: Parables of Poesis.* Lanham, MD: University Press of America, 1997.

Spencer, Herbert. *On Social Evolution: Selected Writings.* Edited by J. D. Peel. Chicago: University of Chicago Press, 1972.

Stace, Christopher. *Gesta Romanorum: A New Translation.* Manchester, UK: Manchester University Press, 2016.

Stein, Dina. Maxims, Magic, Myth: A Folkloristic Perspective of Pirkē de Rabbi Eli'ezer. [In Hebrew.] Jerusalem: Magnes Press, 2004.

Stern, David. "Rhetoric and *Midrash*: The Case of the *Mashal.*" *Prooftexts* 1, no. 3 (1981): 261–91.

Sutton, Dana F. *The Catharsis of Comedy.* Lanham, MD: Rowman & Littlefield, 1994.

Swan Charles. *Gesta Romanorum.* London: G. Bell & Sons, 1905.

Szpiech, Ryan. *Conversation and Narrative: Reading and Religious Authority in Medieval Polemic.* Philadelphia: University of Pennsylvania Press, 2012.

Ta-Shma, Israel. "The Riddle of the Book *Menorat ha-Ma'or* and Its Solution." [In Hebrew.] *Tarbiṣ* 64, no. 3 (1995): 395–400.

Taylor, Archer. "The Biographical Pattern in Traditional Narrative." *Journal of the Folklore Institute* 1 (1964): 114–29.

Thibaudet, Albert. *French Literature from 1789 to Our Era.* Translated by Charles Lam Markmann. New York: Funk & Wagnalls, 1967.

Thomas, Pavel. "Literary Genres as Norms and Good Habits." *New Literary History* 34, no. 2 (2003): 201–10.

Thompson, Stith. *Motif Index of Folk Literature.* Bloomington: Indiana University Press, 1966.

Tishby, Isaiah, and Joseph Dan, comps. *Mivḥar Sifrut ha-Musar: Praqim Nivḥarim be-Ṣēruf Ṣiyunim, Be'urim ve-Mevo'ot* [Selected musar literature]. [In Hebrew.] Tel Aviv: M. Newman, 1970.

Tohar, Vered. *The Book of Tales, Sermons and Legends (Ferrara 1554): An Anthology of Hebrew Stories from the Print Era.* [In Hebrew.] Tel Aviv: Hakibbutz Hameuchad, 2016.

———. "Distribution of Narrative Traditions in Europe and the Middle East: The Products of the Usque Printing House." In *Aliento* 9 (2017): 175–94.

———. "Does Print Matter? The 16th Century Printed Editions of the Hebrew Essay 'Midrash on the Ten Commandments'." In *Aliento* 10 (2018): 413–26.

———. "The Exegesis of Baḥya ben Asher for Gen 15:7." *European Journal of Jewish Studies* 9 (2015): 132–51.

———. "*Midrash 'Aseret ha-Dibrot*': The Ferrara 1554 Edition vs. the Lublin 1572 Printed Editions." [In Hebrew.] In *Reflections on Booklore: Studies Presented to Avidov Lipsker*, edited by Yigal Schwartz, Lilach Nethanel, Claudia Rosenzweig, and Rona Tausinger, 495–508. Ramat-Gan: Bar-Ilan University Press, 2020.

———. "Rabbi Meir and His Friend's Wife." [In Hebrew.] In *Encyclopedia of the Jewish Story: Sippur Okev Sippur*, vol. 3, edited by Yoav Elstein, Avidov Lipsker, and Rella Kushelevsky, 155–80. Ramat-Gan: Bar-Ilan University Press, 2013.

Tolan, Victor. *Petrus Alfonsi and His Medieval Readers*. Gainesville: University Press of Florida, 1993.

Tubach, Frederic. *Index Exemplorum: A Handbook of Medieval Religious Tales*. Helsinki: Suomalainen Tiedeakatemia, 1969.

Urbach, Ephraim E. *The Sages: Their Concepts and Beliefs*. [In Hebrew.] Jerusalem: Magnes, 1986.

Uther, Hans-Jörg. *The Types of International Folktales: A Classification and Bibliography*. Helsinki: Suomalainen Tiedeakatemia, 2004.

Vinograd, Yeshayahu. *Thesaurus of the Hebrew Book*. [In Hebrew.] Jerusalem: Institute for Digital Bibliography, 1994.

Warren, Zev Harvey. "Ethical Theories among Medieval Jewish Philosophers." In *The Oxford Handbook of Jewish Ethics and Morality*, edited by Elliot N. Dorff and Jonathan K. Crane, 84–101. Oxford: Oxford University Press, 2013.

Werses, Shmuel. "Studies on the Musar Literature of the Jews in Spain from the Beginning of the 13th Century to the End of the 15th Century." [In Hebrew.] PhD diss., Hebrew University of Jerusalem, 1947.

Willi, Andeas, ed. *The Language of Greek Comedy*. Oxford: Oxford University Press, 2002.

Wineman, Aryeh. Ethical Tales from the Kabbalah: Stories from the Kabbalistic Ethical Writings. Philadelphia: Jewish Publication Society, 1999.

———. "*Ḥasid* and *Ḥakham*: Paradoxical Stories Found in Cabbalistic Ethical Literature." *Hebrew Studies* 25 (1984): 52–61.

Wise, Stephen Samuel. *The Improvement of the Moral Qualities: An Ethical Treatise of the Eleventh Century by Solomon Ibn Gabirol*. New York: Columbia University Press, 1901.

Wolfson, Elliot R. "The Body in the Text: A Kabbalistic Theory of Embodiment." *Jewish Quarterly Review* 95, no. 3 (2005): 479–500.

Woolf, Jeffrey. "When Was the Book *Orḥot Ṣaddiqim* Written?" [In Hebrew.] *Qiryat Sefer* 64, no. 1 (1993): 321–22.

Yassif, Eli. *Book of Memories: Chronicles of Yeraḥme'el.* [In Hebrew.] Tel Aviv: Tel Aviv University Press, 2001.

———. "The Exemplary Story in *Sefer Ḥasidim.*" [In Hebrew.] *Tarbiṣ* (1988): 220–23.

———. *The Hebrew Folktale: History, Genre, Meaning.* Bloomington: Indiana University Press, 1999.

———. "The Hebrew Narrative Anthology in the Middle Ages." *Prooftexts* 17, no. 2 (1997): 153–75.

———. *Ke-Margalit ba-Mishbetset: Kovets ha-Sippurim ha-'Ivri bi-Yemey ha-Beynayim* [Like a pearl in a slot: A collection of the Hebrew tales in the Middle Ages]. [In Hebrew.] Tel Aviv: Ha-Kibbutz ha-Me'uḥad, 2004.

Zfatman, Sara. *Between Ashkenaz and Sepharad: The Jewish Tale in the Middle Ages.* [In Hebrew.] Jerusalem: Magnes Press, 1993.

Index of Authors, Themes, Literary Figures, and Terms

Note: Page numbers followed by *f* and *t* indicate figures and tables, respectively.

Comedy, xiii, 37–42, 41*t*, 48, 50, 58, 91; Greek, 38–40, 42; vs. tragedy, 37, 38–39, 40, 57, 126n23
Commedia dell'arte, 39
Compassion (virtue), ix, 23, 88
Conduct, 30, 74, 84; *musar* as teaching, xiii, 10, 15, 25, 38, 46, 56, 58, 67*t*, 91, 95, 102, 104; theodicy and, 76, 80; women and, 20, 52–53
Cordovero, Moses b. Jacob, 101
Cruelty (vice), 22, 23
Culi, Ya'akov, 6

"Death of a Scholar's Sons for a Lie," 74–78
Defamiliarization, 89
"Disappointed Farmer, The," 112
Divine justice, 67*t*, 68, 75, 80, 111
"Drowning at Sea," 109
"Drug of Life, The," 88–89

"Elijah and the Bad Smell," 112
Elijah ha-Kohen ha-Itamari, 29, 44, 105–6
Elijah the Prophet (biblical figure; tale character), 48, 50–51, 59, 112
English language, xvi, 4, 55, 101
Envy (vice), 42, 73
Eros (a.k.a. Amor; Greek/Roman character), 19, 28
"*Ēshet Ḥayil.*" *See* "Woman of Valor, A"
Esther (biblical figure, a.k.a. Hadassah), 42, 48
Ethical will, 7, 43–44, 104, 108
Euripides, 22–23
Eurydice (Greek character), 19
Evil, 15, 18, 23, 25, 33, 80, 111, 113, 124n26
"Evil Neighbor, The," 32–33
Exegesis, 47
Exemplum, exempla, 4, 19, 63–67, 67*t*, 73, 76, 127n2
Expulsion of Jews (1492), 7

"Father's Will, The." *See* "Loyal Sons, The"
"Father Who Breastfed His Son, The," 42, 43
"Father Who Was Cursed, The," 110
Fidelity test, 68
Flattery (vice), 67–68
Folklore, 1, 5, 68, 80–81, 88; *musar* literature and, xi–xii, xv, 10–11, 13–14, 63–64, 67, 81, 89, 96
Fool's tale, 12, 73, 86
Forgetfulness (vice), 72
French language, 4, 12, 28, 55

Ga'on, Nissim b. Jacob from Qairouan, 5–6, 55
Ga'on, Sa'adia, 44
Genre, xii, xiii, xvi, 6, 84, 93, 96, 98; *musar* as its own, xv, 10, 78, 95, 96, 97, 129n12. *See also* Allegory; Comedy; Parable; Tragedy
German language, 55
Gerondi, Jonah b. Abraham, 84, 103
"Good Samaritan, The," 88
"Gossip, The," 110
Gozzadini, Tommaso, 105
Greed (vice), 73
"Greedy and the Envious, The," 73
Greek drama, 23, 38; comedy, 38–40, 42; tragedy, 17, 19, 22–23
Greek language, 63, 125n3, 125n13

Habitus, xiii, 25, 65–66, 82
Hadassah. *See* Esther
Ḥagiz, Jacob Israel, 7
Halakhah (practical Jewish law), 56–57, 102
ha-Qadosh, ha-Ari. *See* Luria, Isaac b. Solomon Ashkenazi
Ḥasidism, 14
Haskalah (Jewish Enlightenment movement), 14
Hebrew language, xvi, 87, 95, 101, 102, 117n8
Homer, 45
Honesty (virtue), 17, 74, 75, 78, 105
Horowitz, Abraham b. Shabbetai, 104
"Humble Sage, The," 107
Humility (virtue), 12, 106
Ḥuṣin, Shelomoh Bekhor, 7

Ibn 'Aṭṭar, Ḥayyim b. Mosheh, 7
Ibn Duran, Shim'on b. Ṣemaḥ, 69
Ibn Falaquera, Shem-Ṭov b. Joseph, 69
Ibn Gabirol, Solomon b. Judah, 6, 71–73, 102–3
Ibn Sahula, Isaac b. Solomon, 7
Ibn Tibbon, Judah b. Shaul, 69, 101–2
IFA. *See* Israel Folklore Archive
"Injury, The." *See* "Two Merchants and the Doomed Ship, The"
Innocence, 30–31, 74, 78
"Innocent Man and His Wife, The," 110
Isaac b. Eliakim of Posen, 7
Islamic history and culture, 3, 55, 81, 102, 103
Israel Folklore Archive (IFA), 51
Italian language, 4, 105, 119n17

Jephthah's daughter (biblical figure), 80
Joke, 12, 38, 39, 60
Joy, 54
Judah Aryeh of Modena. *See* Leon of Modena
Judeo-Arabic language, 5–6, 101, 102
Jusepe de Ribera, 43

Kaidanover, Zvi Hirsch, 6, 24, 26, 29, 55, 105
Kindness (virtue), 50, 87–88
"King and the Candle, The," 69–71
"King and the Letter, The." *See* "King Who Was Afraid to Get Angry, The"
"King Who Bestowed Silk, The," 85–86
"King Who Was Afraid to Get Angry, The" (a.k.a. "The King and the Letter"), 71–73
Kook, Avraham Yitzchak Hakohen, 6

Ladino language, 6, 117n8
Lamia (Greek character), 23
Latin language, 3, 4, 12, 28, 63
"Lentils and the Pumpkins, The," 11–12
Leon of Modena, 8, 69, 104
Lilith (character), 23, 127n38
Love of God (virtue), 106, 111
"Loyal Sons, The" (a.k.a. "The Father's Will"), 43–44
Luria, Isaac b. Solomon Ashkenazi (a.k.a. ha-Ari ha-Qadosh), 123n13
Luzzatto, Moshe Ḥaim (a.k.a. Ramḥal), 11, 106

"Maiden Who Jumped Off the Roof, The," 20–22
"Man with One Book, The," 55–57
Marie de France, 28
Matya ben Ḥeresh, 17–18
Medea (Greek character), 22–23
Medusa (Greek character), 19
Meir, Rabbi, 17, 21, 30–31, 76
Menander (Greek character), 39
Metaphor, 39, 64, 66, 69, 82, 85, 97*t*; as path to piety, 11, 103, 104, 106; women and, 19, 28
Metareading, xi, 93
Metasystem, 96, 97
Metatron (tale character), 52–53, 59
Modesty (virtue), 11, 16–17, 26, 69–71
Molière, 39
Mordecai (biblical figure), 42, 48
Moses (biblical figure), 76, 83, 87
Moses b. Naḥman. *See* Naḥmanides
Musar literature, 8, 37–38, 40–41, 46, 58, 79, 89–91, 94–95, 97–99, 97*t*; authors/readership of, 1, 64–66, 76–78, 88; conduct and, xiii, 10, 15, 25, 38, 46, 56, 58, 67*t*, 91, 95, 102, 104; folklore and, xi–xii, xv, 10–11, 13–14, 63–64, 67, 81, 89, 96; as a genre, xv, 10, 78, 95, 96, 97, 129n12
Mysticism, 14, 102, 104, 123n13, 127n35

Naḥmanides (a.k.a. Ramban, or Moses b. Naḥman), 6
Naḥum Ish Gamzu, 3, 54

Odysseus (Greek character), 45, 83
Oedipus (Greek character), 17
Orpheus (Greek character), 19
Orthodox Judaism, 64, 95, 97
Ovid, 22

Papo, Eliezer, 7
Parable, xiii, 6, 85–86, 88, 103, 127n2
Paratext, 64–65, 67*t*, 84, 97, 97*t*
Parsimony (vice), 89
Penelope (Greek character), 45
Perseus (Greek character), 19
"Pious Man and the Soldiers, The," 81–82
Plautus, Titus Maccius, 39
Prayer (virtue), 24–25, 32
"Praying Pious Man and the Bishop, The," 108
Pregnancy, 44, 53–54, 57, 59, 109
"Pregnant Woman and Her Mother, The," 109
"Pretending to Be Mute," 111
Pride (vice), 71, 89
"Prisoner, The," 1–2
"Productive Field, The," 108–9
Psyche (Greek/Roman character), 19, 28
Publius Terentius Afer, 39

"Rabbi and the Calf, The," ix
"Rabbi Meir and His Friend's Wife," 30–31
Ramban. *See* Naḥmanides
Ramḥal. *See* Luzzatto, Moshe Ḥaim
"Raping the Daughter as Punishment," 23–25, 32, 33
Rashi (a.k.a. Shlomo Yiṣḥaqi), 21, 46, 122n6
Reception theory, 65
Remus (Roman character), 42

Romulus (Roman character), 42
Russian formalist school, 89

"Sailor's Wife, The," 84–85
Shakespeare, William, xvi, 4, 39
"Shining Pious Man, The," 111
Shlomo Yiṣḥaqi. *See* Rashi
"Six Good Years," 50–51, 53
"Son Saves His Father in the Afterlife, The," 113
"Stones Outside Your Field," 108

"Tefillin, The," 107
Telemachus (Greek character), 45
Temple, in Jerusalem, 53, 85
Theodicy, 75–76, 80–81
"Three Friends," 114
Torah, 17, 24–25, 44–45, 60, 86, 111, 113
Tragedy, xiii, 15–16, 16*t*, 35, 91; vs. comedy, 37, 38–39, 40, 57, 126n23; Greek, 17, 19, 22–23
Travelogue, 8
Trust (virtue), 28, 51, 68
"Two Merchants and the Doomed Ship, The" (a.k.a. "The Injury"), 54–55

"Ungrateful Child and the Grateful Prisoner, The," 87–88
Uriah (biblical figure), 80

Ventura, Magdalena, 43
Vice, 78, 81, 83, 89, 93, 102–5, 120; anger, 43–44, 47, 48, 71, 89; cruelty, 22, 23; envy, 42, 73; flattery, 67–68; forgetfulness, 72; greed, 73; parsimony, 89; pride, 71, 89; wickedness, 89
"Virgin Who Gouged Out Her Eyes, The," 16–17, 18–19
Virtue, ix, 17, 19, 37, 51, 54, 57, 64, 68, 105; compassion, ix, 23, 88; honesty, 17, 74, 75, 78, 105; humility, 12, 106; kindness, 50, 87–88; love of God, 106, 111; modesty, 11, 16–17, 26, 69–71; prayer, 24–25, 32; trust, 28, 51, 68; vice and, 78, 81, 83, 89, 93, 102–6, 120

Wickedness (vice), 89
"Woman of Valor, A" (*Ēshet Ḥayil*), 51
"Worries Destroy the Heart," 113
"Wrong Grave, The," 111

Yiddish language, 6, 7, 55, 104, 105, 115n1, 117n8, 119n24
Yiṣḥaqi, Shlomo. *See* Rashi

Zeus (Greek character), 23, 42

Index of Biblical and Rabbinic References

Ecclesiastes 9:8 85
Esther 2:10 48
Genesis 1:4, 27 23, 47
  Gen. 2:21–22 23
  Gen. 4:1–15 80
  Gen. 15:7 130n6
  Gen. 18:27 69
  Gen. 25:27 46
Isaiah 55:9 80
Judges 11:31, 34, 39 80
Leviticus 10:1–3 76
Proverbs 12:14 71
  Prov. 31:10–31 51
Psalms 22:7 69
  Ps. 33:13 71
  Ps. 34:13–14 89
  Ps. 74:5 46
  Ps. 140:4 24
  Ps. 145:9 ix
2 Samuel 11:17 80
Avot de-Rabbi Natan 38 126n26
B. Talmud, *'Avodah Zara* 18b 21, 126n26
  Baba Batra 3b 21
  Baba Meṣiah 85a ix
  Bereshit rabbah 30:8 42
  Ketubot 62b 44
  Nedarim 66b 12
  Pesaḥim 2a 46
  Sanhedrin 14a, 97a 74, 126n26
  Shabbat 53a 42
  Ta'anit 21a 126n29
J. Talmud, *Shabbat* 2 46
Mishnah Avot 3:4 46
Pirqē Avot 1:7 124n26
Pirqē Avot 4:1c 82
Qohelet rabbah 9:6 84
Rut Zuṭa 4:11 51
Tanḥuma 122n3
Tanna devē Eliyahu 21 122n7
Vayiqra rabbah 16:2 88
Yalquṭ Shim'oni 126n19

Index of *Musar* Texts and Primary Sources

Page numbers followed by *f* and *t* refer to figures and tables, respectively.

Beḥinat 'olam [The inspection of the world], 101
Brandshpiegel [Burning mirror], 6

Disciplina Clericalis [Teaching the clerics], 3–4

Ēlleh ezkerah [These, I shall remember!], 53

Fiore di Virtu (by Brother Tomasso Gozzadini), 105

Ḥibbur ha-ma'asiyot [Collection of tales], 7
Ḥibbur Yafeh meha-Yeshu'ah [An elegant compilation concerning relief after adversity], 5, 6, 55, 119n18, 123n21, 125n18, 126n30
Ḥovot ha-Levavot [The duties of the hearts], 7, 13*f*, 85, 87, 101

Iggeret ha-Musar [The letter on morality], 69

Kitab al-faraj ba'ad al-shiddah. See *Ḥibbur Yafeh meha-Yeshu'ah*

Ma'agal ṭov [A good round-trip], 8
Ma'alot ha-Middot [The degrees of the virtues], ix, 74, 103, 107
Ma'aseh Nissim [A miraculous tale], 7
Magen Avot [The shield of the Patriarchs], 69
Mashal ha-Qadmoni [The parable of the ancient one], 7
Mayseh Bukh. See *Sefer ha-ma'asim*
Menorat ha-Ma'or [The seven-lamp of light] (by Isaac Aboab), 7, 42, 55, 103–4, 108–10
Menorat ha-Ma'or [Shining candelabra] (by Israel Alnaqua), 7
Meshalim shel Shlomoh ha-Melekh [Fables of King Solomon], 8
Mesillat Yesharim [The path of the upright], 11–12, 90*f*, 106
Midrash 'Aseret ha-Dibrot' [Midrash on the Ten Commandments], 5, 6, 118n14

Mi-Meqor Yisra'el [From the fountain of Israel], 115n2, 127n33
Mishlē Shu'alim [Fox fables], 121n32
Mivḥar ha-Peninim [Selected pearls], 72, 102–3, 110

Nofet ṣufim [Sweet honey], 7

Odyssey (by Homer), 45
Or ha-ḥayyim [The light of life], 7
Orḥot Ṣaddiqim [The ways of the righteous], 32

Pele yo'eṣ [Wonderful advisor], 7

Qav ha-yashar [The just measure], x*f*, 6, 24, 26, 29–30, 55, 105, 111–12

Ṣava'at ha-Ramban [The Ramban's will, a.k.a. The will of Naḥmanides], 6
Ṣava'at R. Yehudah ha-Nasi [The Will of R. Judah ha-Nasi], 7
Ṣe'enah u-re'enah [Come out and look, a.k.a. *Ṣenerene* or *Ṣeno Reno* in Yiddish], 7, 119n24
Sefer ha-ma'alot [The book of steps], 7
Sefer ha-ma'asim [The book of deeds], 8
Sefer Ḥasidim [The book of the pious], 6, 7, 8, 43–44, 45, 47–48
Sefer ha-zikhronot [The book of memories, a.k.a. The chronicles of Jerahmeel], 8
Sefer Lev Ṭov [The book of the good heart], 7
Ṣemaḥ ṣaddiq [Righteous growth], 16–17, 20, 22, 69, 74, 104
Sha'arē Teshuvah [The gates of repentance], 9*f*, 84–85, 103
Shēveṭ Musar [The rod of morality], 29–30, 44, 50–51, 52–53, 105–6, 112–13

Tiqun Middot ha-Nefesh [Rectifying the moral qualities of the soul], 6, 49*f*, 69–71, 77*f*, 102, 113
Tomer Devorah [Deborah's palm tree], 101, 131n2

Yalquṭ me'Am Lo'ez [Anthology from a foreign people], 6
Yesh Noḥalin [There are those who inherit], 1–2, 104, 114

Index of Tale Types and Motifs

AT: Aarne, *The Types of the Folktale*, 133

AT 160, "Grateful Animals and Ungrateful Man," 129n10

AT 550A, "Only One Brother Grateful" (ATU 750D, "God and the Three Brothers"), 129n10

AT 554, "The Grateful Animals" (ATU 554, "The Grateful Animals"), 129n9

AT 555, "The Fisherman and His Wife," 126n22

AT 577, "The King's Tasks," 129n8

AT 880–99, "Fidelity and Innocence," 128n8

AT 920–29, "Clever Acts and Words," 128n9

AT 1380–1404, "The Foolish Wife and Her Husband," 121n39

ATU: Uther, *The Types of International Folktales*, 131n13, 143

Rotunda: Rotunda, *Motif Index of the Italian Novella in Prose*, 124n24, 141

Rotunda *Q557.4, "Lions Do Not Harm the Innocent but Devour the Guilty," 31

ST: Thompson, *Motif Index of Folk Literature*, 31, 68, 122n10, 142

ST B29.1, "Face of Woman, Body of Serpent," 122n10

ST B522.3, "Woman Slandered as Adulteress Is Thrown into Lion Pit," 31

ST H200–299, "Test of Truth," 31

ST H210, "Test of Guilt or Innocence," 31

ST H310–59, "Tests for Suitors," 128n8

ST H335, "Tasks Assigned Suitors, Bride as Prize," 129n8

ST H338, "Faithfulness as Suitor Test," 68

ST H1242, "Youngest Brother Alone Succeeds on Quest," 129n8

ST Q115, "Reward: Any Wish Asked for Will Be Granted," 73

Tubach: Tubach, *Index Exemplorum*, 31, 143

Tubach 58, "Adulteress Attacked by Lion," 31

Tubach 3061, "Lion and Hermit," 31